*Life Under Construction*

# *Life Under Construction*

### Designing a Life You Love

Allison M. Liddle

Allison Liddle Consulting, LLC
Wausau

# Contents

# *Testimonials*

"Allison beautifully captures the journey of change in her book, Life Under Construction. While many people resist change and view it as daunting and overwhelming, Allison helps bring clarity and understanding to this process. She empowers you with her own stories of hope and inspiration and equips you to successfully navigate your own journey ahead. Read this book and you'll never experience your life the same way again!"

– Melissa V. West; International Success Coach, Trainer, Speaker, and Author of *Your Daily W.O.W.* and *Hot Pursuit*, North Carolina

"Life Under Construction will motivate you to design a life you love, and then give you actionable steps to create it. Allison provides practical guidance on dreaming big, setting goals, and how not to build a go-cart!"

– Ria Story; Motivational Leadership Speaker and Author, Georgia

"Personal growth is the key to getting more out of life. This book is a great step-by-step guide to set you up for success. Read this with a notepad and pen in hand as this is a book that will be foundational to your growth."

– Chris Robinson; Founder of R3 Coaching and Certified John Maxwell Speaker, Coach and Trainer, Missouri

"Imagine your dream life for yourself. Now stop imagining. This life can be yours." – Allison Liddle in her new book *Life Under Construction*. "Not only is she living out her dream, she has written a step-by-step outline for designing your best life and teaching us on how to do just that in her new book. I love how Allison leads by example with confidence, courage, and the spirit of truly adding value to others. She wants us to step into our greatness and she shows us the way. Life Under Construction is a must read if you are not where you want to be and seeking more for yourself. Thank you Allison, for inspiring me to take action so I can be my best self!"

– Deb Eslinger; Executive Director of State of North Dakota's Women's Business Center & President's Advisory Council Member John Maxwell Team, North Dakota

"Allison Liddle has put together a terrific piece that not only gives inspiration and insight, but shares her story in a way that we can all relate. Her compilation and guidance provides steps to take and tools to use to make your journey in life the right one for you. Discover how to become aware, be inspired, be intentional, visualize, implement, and succeed."

– Kellie R. George; International Certified Communication and Leadership Speaker and Trainer, Nevada

# *Dedication*

I dedicate this book to my smart, kind, beautiful children, Logan and Avery Hope. Each day I am inspired by you. Thank you for your love; I feel blessed beyond measure to be your Mommy.

# *Introduction*

I first thought about writing this book as I was talking to a friend about how I felt like my life was literally under construction. At the time, my family and I had recently moved to a new city, were in the process of building our dream home, and I had just given birth to our second child. My husband and I were also rebranding our business, and our office, too, was literally under construction. Everywhere I looked, there were construction workers, power tools, dug-up piles of dirt, specs and measurements... in other words, I was surrounded by utter havoc and disarray. On top of all that, I was on a mission to grow myself both personally and professionally. I had just discovered that I have a true passion for helping others empower themselves and was in training to become certified as a John Maxwell Team Member—I love leadership development and helping others achieve their dreams. One day, as I explained to my friend how I was feeling, I thought, "I bet there are other people who feel this same way, too." The best way I could think of to share my story and the lessons I've learned was to write a book.

There are very few universals in life, but change is one of them. Change, planned or otherwise, visits all our lives at some point. Maybe you are starting a new business or career; maybe you've recently married or have started a family; maybe you've just moved to a new city; perhaps you've gone back to school or have begun your retirement. Or maybe you simply decided that enough is enough and you simply want to be a better version of yourself.

Many times, when our lives are changing, we may not know what to do next. Everything gets all jumbled together and we get tangled up in our own chaos before we can even get started. If you're like me, you don't like change *at all* and usually try to resist it as much as you can.

We all go through times in life when we feel like there is no rhyme or reason for what is happening. In these moments, the key is to harness change for the better. Instead of letting ourselves get sucked into the whirlpool of change, we must *design* our lives and steer change toward a specific purpose—toward a life you will love. This will transform change from a chaotic storm into an adventure... one that you'll wake up every day feeling excited about.

If you're ready to harness change in order to better yourself and find your own personal happiness, *Life Under Construction: Designing a Life You Love* is for you. This book will help you discover what you really want—and need—in life to feel fulfilled and happy. I'll help you grow yourself for your journey, gather your thoughts, prepare for detours, conquer the fear of change, re-spark your imagination, and much more.

Get ready to build a new life for yourself, one that you never even knew was possible!

# 1

## *Starting Your Journey*

"If you don't design your own life plan, chances are you'll fall into someone else's plan. And guess what they may have planned for you? Not much." –Jim Rohn

Have you ever gotten into your car and said to yourself, "Where am I going?" I know I have. I've actually had to sit there for a moment, behind the wheel, while I figured out my destination.

It's the same with our lives. You need to start to thinking about where your life journey is going to take you, as well as map out the best route you can use to get there. You may have a very clear picture of your destination, but if you're anything like I was two years ago, you don't. All you have is a fuzzy picture of where you think you might want to end up.

*Life Under Construction: Designing a Life You Love* is based on a period in my life when everything seemed to be under construction, both literally and figuratively. In the midst of all that change, I realized that I needed a better plan—something really solid. I needed a plan that was based on my own vision for myself. I took all the chaos around me and harnessed it. By sharing my story, I hope that you'll be able to learn how to design your own life—a life you will love.

The reason we embark on designing a life that we love is different for each of us. For me, I was ready for a change, even though I admit I'm usually adverse to change. I was excited about the possibility of living a new life. I was intrigued to see what would happen if I stopped listening to all of my own excuses about why I couldn't accomplish something; instead, I started believing in all of the reasons why I could succeed.

The journey to creating a new life is never easy—this is why so many people give up, even if they had the best intentions at the start. When things become too difficult or problematic, many of us sink back into our old ways of doing things. I'll admit that throughout my journey I've experienced days when I wanted my old life back, but then I'd remember my commitment to myself. I'd then do the exact opposite of what the "old me" would've done. So far, it has worked marvelously.

When I started writing this book, I had no idea what I would come up with, but I was enthusiastic anyhow. I had faith that if I shared my experiences, others would find value in the life lessons I've learned.

§

When you are starting off on any journey, you need to know where you are going—which can sometimes be the most difficult part. That's why you need to take some time to figure out where you're trying to go. I was lucky to have realized this early on in my journey, so I was able to spend some time exploring myself. You need to do the same so you can start understanding yourself on a deeper level: a level deeper than you've probably ever explored. I've heard that if you don't know your purpose in life, it will be difficult to feel as though you are truly accomplishing anything. Judging from my own experiences, this is true.

When your life is under construction, you need to start building your foundation first. A house without a strong foundation might be beautiful, but it won't be structurally sound: the same is true with life-design. The foundation for designing a life you will love is increasing your self-awareness. In order to create a life that is stable, you must start by understanding yourself better: Are you an introvert or an extrovert? Are you a big-picture thinker or detail oriented? What are your strengths? What do you dislike doing? If you could do something all day long and get lost in it, what would it be? These are important things to start identifying about yourself.

One tool that may help you identify your traits is a personality test. There are many great personality tests out there, but the ones I like the best are the StrengthsFinder 2.0, and the VIA Survey, both of which are well recognized in the industry. Both are available online, and the StrengthsFinder quiz, in particular, can give you a comprehensive report on your strengths. If you have access to a Myers-Briggs Type Indicator test that would be wonderful too. If you've never taken a personality test before, you'll probably be shocked by what you learn. After looking over your results, I bet you'll recognize things about yourself that you never consciously knew before.

For example, one of my friend's personality strengths is harmony, which essentially means he likes to create peace in his life. He does *not* like conflict—so much so that he intentionally and deliberately avoids it. After he took his personality test and saw harmony listed as one of his strengths, he told me that harmony was something he had always disliked about himself—he felt he was always trying to please others, almost to a fault. But as he read more about harmony, he came to realize that he used this trait, both at home and at work, to keep others happy and help find them common ground.

As for myself, I was shocked when I learned that two of my strengths are being strategic and being creative. When I got my results, I had an "ah-ha!" moment—I finally realized why I was always creating strategic plans in my spare time. I thought it was a quirk that I had, but after getting my results, I realized that I was usually a couple steps ahead of others and that I liked creating plans so I could implement my ideas effectively. When I saw "innately creative" listed among my test results, I recognized this in myself instantly, yet also knew that I didn't have an outlet in my life for that creativity. No wonder I felt so drained of energy!

After you receive your personality test results, you will start to identify things about yourself that you probably always knew on some level, but now you'll be able to evaluate them with a more critical eye. You are important: taking time out of your busy schedule to understand more about yourself is a foundational part of your journey. If you never take the time to understand yourself better, you won't be able to build your foundation—never mind the rest of your life.

Begin by thinking about the top three to five strengths revealed in your personality test(s), and ask yourself these questions about each: What do I think about this strength? Am I utilizing this strength in my personal life or in my business? If so, how? If not, why not? How can I use my strengths to create greater personal fulfillment?

During this process, it's also important to think about your weaknesses. Identify your top three weaknesses. Sometimes it's helpful to discuss these with your spouse or a close friend—someone who is truly caring and loving toward you. After identifying your weaknesses, ask yourself how they are affecting your life. For example, you may hate mundane details, yet have a job where all you do is fill out paperwork. Or perhaps you love to be around people, but you're stuck in an office all day long where you can't really interact with others. As you identify your weaknesses, often your strengths will emerge. By recognizing this, you can start moving toward the areas in your strength zone—the stuff that you will actually enjoy doing.

Another important step in building your foundation is writing the story of your life. Don't worry, this doesn't have to be a literary masterpiece, just a reflection on yourself. I suggest you begin by creating a life-timeline that starts from your childhood and marks all of the major events in your life. As you review your timeline, write down the answers to some simple, yet meaningful, questions. Questions to get you started include: What were the high points of my life? What were the low points?

What did I learn during these times? What do I love to do? Who do I love to do those things with? What was I like as a child? What did I want to be when I grew up? Am I doing that today? If not, why not?

Everyone has moments when they start to recognize their priorities. I call these "God moments," but you can call them meaningful life moments, or whatever term you prefer. I think these moments are important to note in your life story as well. One of my mentors says that reflecting on our most important experiences is essential to self-growth. Luckily, I had a number of God moments early in life that taught me a lot about myself and my priorities. When I reflect on my God moments, I ask myself these questions, among others.

- What happened? What was unique about this moment?
- When did it happen? How old was I? Who was involved?
- What did I learn from the experience?

## My God Moment: The Airplane Trip that Changed My Life

One of the most terrifying moments in my life was also one of the greatest blessings I've ever received. I was flying home after a job interview. Not just any job interview, but an interview for my dream job. The position was everything I ever wanted for myself professionally, plus it was in a dynamic, exciting city, and my office would be in a beautifully designed skyscraper. I'd received the job offer on the spot. As I flew back home to Wisconsin, I began daydreaming about all the ways in which this job would change my life for the better.

Suddenly, the plane jerked, then dropped in midair. It happened again. Then a third time. Then more times than I could count. This wasn't just turbulence, this was a constant jerking; we were being jolted back and forth, up and down. We'd been caught in a rare thunder-snowstorm as we were flying over Minneapolis, and I was sure I was falling to my demise.

As I frantically scanned the cabin for someone with answers about what was happening, the lights went out. Then nothing. In the darkness, we continued to fall, jerk, then fall some more. Sitting there in the dark, as the plane was tossed back and forth by the storm, everything felt surreal. I saw panic in the eyes of the other passengers. I was terrified.

I didn't know what to do, so I began praying. "Dear God, I just want to get home safely to see my family," I pleaded. "Please, please, let me get home to them. If you get me home safely, I'll even have a baby... wait, two babies. They'll be named Hope and Faith... Okay middle names. And I'll stop asking you for so much... I'll find the happiness in my life."

For the next half hour, the plane continued to jostle. I prayed that prayer over and over again. During those thirty minutes, I had a God moment: I experienced a moment of clarity unlike ever before. In that God moment, I learned three things that forever shaped my life.

1. My family is my number one priority. I realized it doesn't matter where I live or what job I have: as long as I can be with my family, I'll be okay.
2. I wanted to be a mom. My husband and I had been holding off on having children until I found

my dream job, but as we fell mid-air, I realized that I wanted children soon—not "someday."

3. I needed to be more positive and learn to *not* control everything. In the blink of an eye, my life nearly came to an end. I resolved to embrace every day as the gift it actually is. I didn't have to waste my energy worrying about every little thing. All I needed to do was get through each day with a positive attitude.

As we started to break through the clouds and I finally saw the ground below, a sense of calm came over me. We landed roughly and I looked out the window. There were fire trucks, ambulances, and police cars lined up along the tarmac. I think they had anticipated my worst fear, but thankfully we were safe.

I didn't take the job, and not just because I couldn't bring myself to get back on an airplane for a long, long time. Instead, I found an awesome job closer to my family where I was able to help many young children and families.

Today, I have two children—Logan who is now five years old, and Avery Hope who is two years old. They are wonderful little humans and they are amazing blessings in my life. Now, each day I intentionally spend time or talk with my family, love my children unconditionally, and try to approach my life with a positive attitude.

That airplane trip changed everything for me. I gained clarity on what I needed in my life, who I wanted in my life, and what I should do each day. I challenge each of you to visualize your own airplane ride. Think about those people that you can't live without, even those who you may not have met yet. Figure out what in life makes your heart sing: resolve to do more of that. We're all busy and we all have obligations, but make time for yourself, too. Find ways of incorporating your passions into your everyday life.

I shared this story to give you an example of what you may want to focus on when you sit down and begin writing your own life story. Your life story doesn't necessarily have to be linear, and it doesn't have to include every detail of your life. Begin with one of the life-changing moments on your timeline and simply write down everything that comes into your mind. Don't edit things out. As you are writing, you may remember things you haven't thought about in years. You may start to see new connections between past experiences. I know I did.

## Designing Your Life: Questions for Starting Your Journey

Many times, people dive into self-improvement without ever reflecting about where they've been and who they are. I encourage you to stop and think about yourself. Begin with the basics. These early questions may seem obvious, but take the time to answer them anyway; you might be surprised by what you find.

1. Where did I grow up?

2. Who is my family?

3. What type of child was I?

4. What did I love to do as a child?

As you move forward, you can begin answering some larger questions. Refer to your timeline as you answer these; they will help you figure out your starting point.

1. Have I had any life-changing moments? What did I realize after my life-changing events?

2. What are the high points of my life? What are some of the low points?

3. What do I like? What do I hate?

4. What are some of the most important lessons I've learned in life?

You have now started your journey. Congratulations!

# 2

*Preparing to
Design Your Life*

"Some people succeed because they are destined to,
but most people succeed because they are
determined to." —Henry Van Dyke

Now that you have reflected on your life, you're ready for
the next step on your journey: preparing to design your
life. I know that many of us often don't take the time to
prepare for things. So many people prefer to just "go with
the flow" or "see what happens." I even read an online
meme that said, "My life didn't go as planned and that's
ok." In some instances it can be fun to "float along" and
see what happens, but not when you are serious about
designing a life you will love. I'm not going to lie, building
a life that inspires and excites you is going to take a lot of
work, including prep work. That work begins with your

making the decision to immerse yourself in designing your life. I encourage you to give yourself time to go through the entire process. If you do, I can almost guarantee that you will make some significant positive changes in your life.

## Preparation

In 2015, my husband and I decided we would build our own home. It was a big step for us, and I knew we would have a long road ahead. There were countless details to take care of, from the big stuff like financing, to the little things like choosing paint colors.

We began by gathering the tools that would help us to succeed. We purchased a piece of land, took estimates from builders, researched home layouts and designs, decided on materials, and—most importantly—we put ourselves in the right frame of mind before starting the building process. All of these things helped prepare us for the home we knew we wanted. If we had simply started building the house without preparation, we would have been setting ourselves up for failure.

Designing a life you love works the same way. Preparation is key to your success. Some of the things you should gather to prepare for designing your life include a journal, pens (colorful), and a space to think. You will also need to schedule time for yourself to do the exercises in this book, reflect on your attitude, and focus on your needs and what you really want from life. The following three steps will get you started.

## Steps to Prepare For Designing Your Life

1. Reflect: Many times, when you begin a new project you just want to get moving. But after you've decided that you're going to tackle a project, it's crucial that you take some time to think about it. I've heard that many people spend more time planning their family vacation than they do thinking about their life-plans. Isn't that sad? I think so. Schedule time in your busy life to reflect and think things through.

2. Brainstorm: There are many types of brainstorming, but my favorite—and the one I recommend the most—is called a "brain dump." A brain dump is when you simply listen to yourself and write down every idea that comes to mind. Every single idea. It takes patience and discipline to listen to all of those ideas, and persistence to stop and write them down whenever and wherever they come to you. Many of my strongest ideas come to me when I'm taking a shower, or when driving. Some of my absolute best ideas wake me up in the middle of the night. If you don't capture your ideas as soon as they come to you, there's a good chance that you'll never remember them. Keep *Post-it* notes next to your bed, or record your ideas in the notes app on your smartphone. Brainstorming is a process. Your best idea probably won't be the first idea you come up with. After you've been thinking about something for long enough, though, you may find that your mind will begin refining your idea.

3. Gather tools: The tools I use when I'm starting a project are: a beautiful binder, binder dividers, paper, colored pens, *Post-it* notes, a calendar, and a journal. I title

my binder with the name of my project; for your binder, you can download the *Designing My Life* template on my website, www.allisonliddle.com. Once my binder is labeled, I begin thinking about the various sections I need to create inside it.

I have always liked starting new projects. As a child, I would become excited when my teacher would announce that we had a huge project coming up. I'd look around the classroom to see what my classmates thought about the assignment, and never really understood their looks of dread. After school, I would think about the upcoming assignment as I walked home. The newness, the challenge, was exciting to me. I like to be creative and have always approached projects with a creative thought process.

The creative process is a little bit different for everyone, but every creative process has one thing in common: the first try always stinks. That's okay. For me, the creative thought process goes something like this: I come up with an idea. I start brainstorming about all of the possible ways I could implement my idea. I sketch out a first draft, but it turns out terrible—so bad that I'd never show it to anyone, ever. I start to question my first idea. Sometimes I even start feeling pretty dumb and wonder how I ever thought I could achieve my idea.

If you hit this wall, know you are headed in the right direction. I know this seems counterintuitive, but it's not. I was recently at a conference with Seth Godin, the author of *Purple Cow*, and he said we should celebrate our bad ideas. He recommended that we actually write down ten bad ideas every single day because good ideas can appear from bad ones.

During the creative process, when you feel like all you

have are bad ideas, hold on for a little bit longer. I promise, you will come up with a magnificent solution as the "how to" part of the idea emerges from the chaos of your failed first attempts. I have approached many projects this way—whether they were in marketing, graphic design, or even when writing this book. Every time I found myself facing utter frustration, a breakthrough would follow shortly afterward. Things that seemed chaotic would start making sense, and often, parts of my initial terrible designs helped me to determine what I did or didn't want to include in the final project. My first bad idea always helps lead me to a new direction. And what emerges, eventually, is always fabulous. It will be the same for you.

## Prepare Yourself for Failures and Challenges

A big part of designing your new life is resolving to be open to the creative process... and, as with any form of creativity, this involves overcoming the fear of failure. Everyone has failure-fears: what you choose to do with them will ultimately define your success. Remember that even successful people fear failure. I recently heard a very accomplished entrepreneur speak. He has started six different businesses, yet he said that he felt fearful at the start of each and every one of them. It's okay to feel fearful; it's part of the process.

When you are not sure how something is going to turn out, fear may try to hold you back, but don't give in. You have to be willing to fail in order to succeed. In fact, failing may be the very thing that ultimately leads you to success. This is called "failing forward," and it happens more often than you probably think. Look at these examples of failing forward: all of the following are excerpted from The

University of Kentucky's *But They Did Not Give Up* webpage. (1)

- Thomas Edison: As an inventor, Edison made 1,000 unsuccessful attempts at inventing the light bulb. When a reporter asked, "How did it feel to fail 1,000 times?" Edison replied, "I didn't fail 1,000 times. The light bulb was an invention with 1,000 steps."
- Henry Ford failed and went broke five times before he succeeded.
- Vince Lombardi: An expert said of Vince Lombardi: "He possesses minimal football knowledge and lacks motivation." Lombardi, one of the greatest Green Bay Packers' football coaches of all time would write, "It's not whether you get knocked down; it's whether you get back up."
- J.K. Rowling: Twelve publishers rejected J.K. Rowling's book about a boy wizard before a small London house picked up *Harry Potter*.
- Vincent van Gogh sold only one painting during his life. And this was to the sister of one of his friends (for about $50). This didn't stop him from completing over 800 paintings.
- Michael Jordan was cut from his high school basketball team for lack of skill.

[1] Supporting information at https://www.uky.edu/~eushe2/Pajares/OnFailingG.html

All of these successful people experienced "failures" and setbacks. You, too, will inevitably meet some failures or problems during the process of designing a life you will love. This is to be expected. It's okay. The challenges are part of the creative process—they help you figure out what doesn't work and allow you the opportunity to solve setbacks creatively.

One of my favorite books by Andy Andrews is called *Storms of Perfection*. The book is a collection of letters from fifty successful people; one of the book's most common themes is that all of the contributors experienced problems, especially when they were trying to attempt something new in their lives. The passage below is one of Andy's reflections on the many obstacles his contributors faced.

[T]hese problems occurred at various stages in their lives and manifested themselves in a number of ways. Rejection, illness, poverty, self-doubt, imprisonment were on the long list I complied.

But surely, I thought, problems can't be the only factor involved in attaining greatness. Problems in and of themselves couldn't lead directly to success, could they? The answer is obviously no, of course not. These people all eventually found the winner's circle because they refused to quit looking! They didn't shy away from obstacles the way most of us do. They found a way around, tunneled through, or simply kept chipping away at the obstacle until it was no longer there!

Essentially, what Andy is telling us is that pushing

through challenges is how greatness emerges! Remember, even though you will face failures on your journey, you are failing *forward.*

After going through the creative process—and probably hitting a few walls—you may begin wondering why on earth you chose to start designing a life for yourself. After all, prep is a lot of work, which is why most people don't take the time to do it. One way to help yourself get through the creative process is to practice self-care.

I was recently on a phone call with one of my coaches and mentors, Melissa West. She is a wonderful leader, entrepreneur, and author, and, since she grew up in Wisconsin like me, she is also a Cheesehead. I was explaining to her some of the changes that I saw myself making in the near future and I asked her for her advice. She had lots of good ideas to share, but above all she encouraged me to take care of myself both physically and emotionally. She told me to practice self-care so I would be in a healthy, positive frame of mind for the changes ahead.

I'd never really thought about preparing myself for change. "What does that mean?" I thought. Then I remembered many times in my past when I dived into my latest idea head-on: I did nothing to prepare myself, and I definitely never gave self-care a fleeting thought.

Some of my projects worked out well, others did not. After talking with Melissa, I began wondering what would have happened if I had taken a little extra time to care for myself before, and during, some of my less-successful projects. What would have happened if took the time to reflect on what I needed to do to keep myself in a positive mind-set? If I'd taken the time to care for myself, maybe some of my toughest moments wouldn't have been so hard—I would have had the energy and the positive frame of mind to better deal with those twists and turns.

I'm going to encourage you to think about what you need to do to practice self-care. Self-care must be intentional and immersive. There are many tools you can use for self-care:

- Physical: Do you exercise? If not, can you schedule regular exercise sessions while you are designing a life you will love?
- Mental: We all need ways of addressing negative thoughts. For example, if negative thoughts flood your mind every night when your head hits the pillow, try writing them down so that you can fall asleep more peacefully.
- Daily Positivity: A positive mind-set is crucial. Write yourself encouraging notes and post them around your home as reminders. Try listening to upbeat, positive music. In your free moments, try watching affirming TED Talks or YouTube videos. Write a thank-you card to yourself every day to thank yourself for everything that you did; on the tough days, you can open the cards to remind yourself how awesome you are!

Remember that self-care is not selfish. So often we put everyone else's needs ahead of our own, but self-care helps us to be at our best, and that means we will have that much more to give to others—especially when we are facing life changes.

# Designing Your Life: Questions for Preparing to Design Your Life

Just like when you're starting a construction project, it is important that you prepare yourself to design your life. Start with the basics, like a *Designing My Life* binder. As you come up with notes and ideas, put these into your binder. Remember, designing a life you will love involves perseverance, creativity, and your very best ideas.

1. Did I make the *Designing My Life* binder by going to www.allisonliddle.com and downloading the template? Have I collected the following tools?
    1. Binder
    2. Dividers
    3. Paper
    4. Pens (colorful)
    5. Post-it notes

2. Have I made time for reflection and brainstorming? If not, how can I schedule this? Do I have a designated space for reflection? If not, where can I focus best?

3. When have I failed? What did I learn from these experiences? How can I fail forward in my life?

4. How will I practice self-care while I am designing my life? What things can I do to make sure that I'm in the best frame of mind for the changes ahead?

Congratulations, you're on your way! Preparation is the key to success!

# 3

*Understanding*
*Change*

"The secret of change is to focus all of your energy,
not on fighting the old, but on building the new."
—Socrates

Now that you've done some initial prep work, you are well
on your way to designing a life you will love. Are you
getting excited yet? Your life is officially under
construction. You're still in the designing stages, but
nonetheless, you're on your way!

What does it mean to have your life under
construction? That's a great question. When my life was
under construction, it felt a lot like the literal building
of my new home. When my husband and I initiated the
building process, we had two options: one was to plan
out our new home carefully, with intention and purpose,

while the other was to just "wing it," make decisions on the fly, and see what happened. I'll bet there are some people who have taken the latter route to building a home, and my guess is that their houses are not still standing. Another, more effective way to build a house is to plan out the entire process in advance. I started by considering all that I needed and wanted in my new home, then designed it on paper. Then I began finding the best contractors and construction crews to do the physical building, while also carefully planning for related issues surrounding financing, zoning laws, and permits. Your life under construction will be a lot like this.

Right now, as you begin designing a life you will love, you are in the first phases of a life under construction. To be successful, you need to have two key pieces to the puzzle: you have to have the knowledge that you are in the construction process, and you need to create a plan for that construction.

I will admit I have always hated change. Despised it, actually. Most people prefer not to change. I've heard that people will change only when the pain of staying the same is greater than the pain of changing. This was certainly true for me. My husband and I were both born and raised in northern Wisconsin. We both went off to college in Michigan, but then came right back home after graduation. We had bought our house right after we got married, and had lived there ever since. The little community we lived in was all we had ever known.

After my daughter was born in 2015, my husband and I did this huge thing: we moved south. By "south" I mean an hour and a half away, but for us, this was a giant step outside of our comfort zone. We had been talking about moving for months, even years, but for one reason or another, we would always sink back into our comfortable world and stay put. With the arrival of Avery, our second child, the pain of staying where were finally outweighed the risks of moving—otherwise we might still be in our hometown.

When my daughter was born, a whole bunch of things in our life changed. The first and most important of these was that Avery was born about one month early. Thankfully, just prior to her birth, we had switched from our local doctor to a physician who was at an advanced medical center in central Wisconsin. The new doctor's office was about an hour and a half south of our home.

Our experience with the new hospital and doctor was wonderful, and we felt all the more secure because the new hospital had a neonatal intensive care unit (NICU) for preemies. We never realized how important access to a NICU was to our family until Avery was born early: we'd never thought about how critical it could be—potentially a matter of life or death—for a premature infant to have her healthcare needs met in a moment of crisis. This was a scary realization. If we had delivered Avery at our local hospital, and if anything had gone wrong with her birth, a helicopter would have had to transfer her to the NICU.

We were blessed that Avery never did need NICU treatment, but, as parents, this was a wake-up call. Health care for our children was critical; we needed access to better options. As we drove out of the hospital with our new tiny baby, we saw a sign—literally, a sign. It was an advertisement for an upcoming parade of homes. My husband and I looked at each other and asked, "Hey, do you think we should go?" That one decision initiated so much change in our lives inside of one year that I can still hardly believe it.

We sold our house in northern Wisconsin, moved away from the only community we'd ever known, and found ourselves in a rental house in a brand-new city. It's hard to explain how much of my life was on autopilot until we moved—I just never realized how many day-to-day things we took for granted. We had to relearn how to do just about everything in our new city. For example, I had to learn where to do the grocery shopping, figure out where the pharmacy was, and map out all the nearest convenience stores. All this newness was disorienting, frightening. I was going through all of this tremendous change, but wanting desperately to just go back to my old life. My comfortable, familiar life.

Change comes in all different shapes and sizes. Some change is small, like buying a new shirt or getting a new haircut. These changes are the type of change we don't think about much—the easy, mundane stuff that comes in tiny increments. Other changes—like moving, starting a new career, getting married, going to college, or having a baby—are big, and they take us way out of our comfort zones. Big changes do more than alter something in your life, they transform you into someone different. They make you grow as a person, and you really can't go back to the way your life used to be after the change. Big changes push us to do more with our lives; they're uncomfortable and scary, and they certainly don't make us feel warm and fuzzy inside. In fact, they do the opposite—they overwhelm us, cause us to self-doubt, and can even make us feel inferior.

So, why then does anyone ever make these big changes? It doesn't sound like fun at all. Why not just stay exactly where you are? Why not keep doing exactly the same thing you have always done, day in and day out?

Think about it: if you never changed, you'd never grow, never learn, never take advantage of your potential or what life really has to offer. This is why we make big changes, even though change can be hard.

## Charting Change

### CHART A: *Emotions Connected to Change*

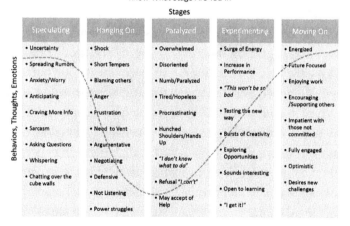

**In Times of Change, Complexity and Uncertainty**
Know What Stage Are You In

| | Stages | | | |
|---|---|---|---|---|
| **Speculating** | **Hanging On** | **Paralyzed** | **Experimenting** | **Moving On** |
| • Uncertainty | • Shock | • Overwhelmed | • Surge of Energy | • Energized |
| • Spreading Rumors | • Short Tempers | • Disoriented | • Increase in Performance | • Future Focused |
| • Anxiety/Worry | • Blaming others | • Numb/Paralyzed | | • Enjoying work |
| • Anticipating | • Anger | • Tired/Hopeless | • *"This won't be so bad* | • Encouraging /Supporting others |
| • Craving More Info | • Frustration | • Procrastinating | • Testing the new way | • Impatient with those not committed |
| • Sarcasm | • Need to Vent | • Hunched Shoulders/Hands Up | • Bursts of Creativity | |
| • Asking Questions | • Argumentative | | • Exploring Opportunities | • Fully engaged |
| • Whispering | • Negotiating | • *"I don't know what to do"* | • Sounds interesting | • Optimistic |
| • Chatting over the cube walls | • Defensive | • Refusal *"I con't"* | • Open to learning | • Desires new challenges |
| | • Not Listening | • May accept of Help | • *"I get it!"* | |
| | • Power struggles | | | |

*(Y-axis label: Behaviors, Thoughts, Emotions)*

## CHART B: *Two Emotion Curves*

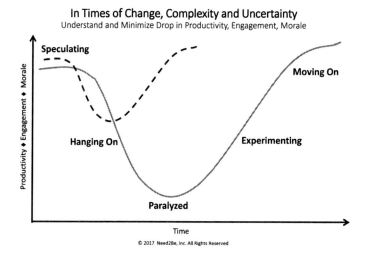

**In Times of Change, Complexity and Uncertainty**
Understand and Minimize Drop in Productivity, Engagement, Morale

I received Chart A from my former supervisor, Bruce Mayle, who was the superintendent of an intermediate school district in upper Michigan. The chart was designed by Katy Caschera founder and CEO of Need2Be. My supervisor had received the change chart at a professional development meeting. I always enjoyed discussing the concepts he learned at these meetings, and one afternoon we started talking about this chart. I've had it on the wall in my office ever since. I've read hundreds of self-development books, yet I've never seen another chart that describes the stages of change so simply yet accurately. I find this chart so incredibly helpful that I wanted to share it with all of you; Katy generously granted permission to reprint it here.

Chart B is also of Katy's design; I find this chart just as helpful as the first. The following excerpt, also reprinted with permission, is how Katy explains the stages shown in her Chart B:

## Personal Success in a Constantly Changing World

*by Katy Caschera, President, Need2Be, Inc. (Helping individuals, teams and organizations thrive today and tomorrow)/©2017 Need2Be, Inc. All Rights Reserved.*

In today's world of constant change, increasing complexity, and ongoing uncertainty, personal success is directly related to a person's resiliency or ability to effectively and efficiently deal with change and adversity at home, work, and in every aspect of life. The key to improving resiliency is to understand the normal stages we all move through as we face change and know what to do to help ourselves move through these stages more efficiently and effectively.

Anytime we face a change, our morale, productivity, and engagement drops. (See chart B.) The dark line represents the typical stages we go through when we face a change. During the first stage, when we first hear about a change, we start speculating. We may ask ourselves, "What exactly is happening and how is this going to affect me?" Once we understand the details of the change and how it will affect us, we show our feelings and demonstrate our frustrations by complaining, arguing, being short tempered, and talking incessantly about how our lives will be impacted. We resist any change by **hanging on** to the old way. During the third stage, we are at the bottom of the curve. Here we often feel overwhelmed and **paralyzed** and unable to do much of anything. We are at a low point in morale, productivity, and engagement. As we move into the fourth stage we realize it might not be that bad or at least we feel more confident in our ability to handle the change and begin **experimenting** with ways to deal with the change in a positive way. During the fifth stage, we are back to feeling good, being productive, and engaging with others. We are **moving on!**

People move through these stages at a certain speed and intensity. The bold, solid curve in the chart represents a person who is not very resilient. This person will experience intense feelings and demonstrate low morale, low productivity, and low engagement longer than someone who is more resilient as shown with the dotted line. The resilient person will, often unnoticeably, move quickly through the stages and will experience a minimal drop in their morale, productivity, and engagement and thereby move through life experiencing more success and joy. In our constantly changing world we all need to be more resilient.

You can increase your resiliency by knowing what to do to help yourself move through the stages of change more quickly and minimize the drop in your morale, productivity, and engagement. In the first stage, as you begin to speculate, **seek out information** that will help you fully understand the change. Whether you receive positive or negative information about how this change will affect you, in the second stage you will want to find someone you trust to just vent or **talk it through.**

Talking about all your feelings can be exhausting and will push you into the bottom of the curve or that third stage. Here you will feel overwhelmed, exhausted and will have the lowest morale, productivity, and engagement. During this stage, it is essential you **ask others for help and direction** in prioritizing your life and getting you doing something productive. As you start to feel yourself gaining your morale, productivity, and engagement levels, you will gain confidence that you can deal with the change. There is light at the end of the tunnel! You are on the up curve! Jump in and do whatever it takes to **adjust** your attitude and behaviors to accommodate the change. When you are feeling your *normal* self again **recognize and reward** your accomplishment and be prepared for the next change to come.

In this constantly changing world we all need to learn to be more resilient. Be aware of the normal stages of dealing with change and help push yourself through these stages quickly to minimize a drop in productivity, engagement, and morale. In doing so you will be able to enjoy more personal success! Be prepared for constant change. Improve your ability to adapt and move on. Be resilient!

Understanding change is so key to navigating your life under construction. Whenever I am facing a change, I can look at this chart and identify the stage of change I am in. Recognizing where I am on the chart offers me clarity about my emotions and helps me recognize what is coming next. For example, I know that after paralysis comes experimenting. Or, when I feel a surge of energy, I know that I'm moving on toward great things. Remember to recognize that change can be a good thing.

## Designing Your Life: Questions for Understanding Change

Life is full of changes. As you begin designing a new life for yourself, you will experience change, which will be scary sometimes. Because you did your prep work, you now probably have some insights into what you want from your new life, and you've also started a self-care ritual to help ground you as your life changes. Now it's time to identify some of the emotions you may experience while your life is under construction. By anticipating and understanding your emotions, you'll be able to push yourself outside of your comfort zone as you design a life you love!

1. What do I think about change?


2. Is it easy or hard for me to change?


3. When were times in my life when I needed to change? What did I learn?

4.  Is it easy for me to start something new? When I start something new, does it energize me or frighten me?

5.  What are some of the ways that I've succeeded in the past?

6.  What is my comfort zone? Where do I live? What do I do? What are my hobbies?

7.  Do I actively seek out opportunities to bring myself outside of my comfort zone?

8.  Can I identify where I am right now on the change chart?

9.  Can I identify with any of the behaviors or emotions related to the stage I identified in Question 8?

Taking time to understand change and how it can impact your life is a really important step that will help you to move forward. Congratulations on recognizing how important change is in your life!

# 4

## *Grow for Your Journey*

**"The first step toward success is taken when you refuse to be a captive of the environment in which you first find yourself." —Mark Caine**

Imagine your dream life for yourself. It will be a better life than you have ever previously envisioned. When you look at yourself in the mirror, your reflection will be different. You'll be in shape physically, and you'll and exude confidence. From the inside, you'll feel different, too, because you'll no longer be problem-focused—your thinking will now be solution-focused. Instead of challenges, you'll see opportunities. Each day, you will be intentional and mindful about how you spend your time and energy, rather than constantly in flux.

In your dream life, you'll be focused on something you

love doing. You may be in the process of building a new business or starting a new career, but in any case, your life will be filled with new things that you almost never thought could happen... but then you will realize that, yes, these amazing things are happening to *you*. What's more, you'll understand that you *deserve* these things. You'll start attracting fantastic opportunities. Many things in your dream life will be different, but above all, you'll know that you're on the right path.

Now stop imagining. This life can be yours.

In his book *The 15 Invaluable Laws of Growth*, John Maxwell says, "It's possible to change without growing, but it's impossible to grow without changing." We must find ways of making positive changes in our lives, the types of changes that allow us to grow. One key aspect of this is understanding the difference between an issue or a challenge, which can be changed, and a fact of life, which cannot be changed.

Another thing I learned from *The 15 Invaluable Laws of Growth* is that we must learn to live with certain unchangeable facts about ourselves. There are some things we simply have no control over, and never will. You will never be able to change your birthplace. You're stuck with your DNA, whether you like it or not. You'll never be able to grow six inches taller. But so what? Wishing away facts about ourselves is wasted energy. However, what you *can* change is your attitude about your life facts. Life facts can't be changed, but designing a life you will love isn't defined by the stuff you can't change, but rather by what you choose to do with the things you *can* change.

John Maxwell also tells us that one of the ways to judge whether you're growing effectively is to discern whether you're looking *forward* to the things yet to come, or looking *back* at what you've already done. If you're not looking forward, it's time to so think about the types of activities and environments you find to be nurturing; this will help you create a more positive environment for your growth. At the end of this chapter, you will find a list of questions excerpted from *The 15 Invaluable Laws of Growth*. Answering these questions will help you to identify what nurtures you personally.

Part of figuring out what nurtures you is examining the relationships in your life. Jim Rohn, an entrepreneur, and author, once said, "You are the average of the five people you spend the most time with." When you're taking big risks and creating a new, fabulously awesome life for yourself, you may begin to see who in your life is truly supportive, and who is not. Your social circle at work, which probably includes at least a few people you've been having after-work drinks with for years, may not understand your new life ambitions, and maybe an unmistakable distance will grow between you. Maybe even members of your family will start to see the changes you are making in your life and misunderstand you. Some people may even do things to try to sabotage your growth. It's sad and sometimes difficult, but, unfortunately, an unchangeable life- fact is that some people will not, or cannot, support you as you grow.

Part of the reason change is so hard is because it doesn't just affect us, it affects those around us as well. As you step outside of your comfort zone, the positive changes you initiate will become obvious. This may make others take a good hard look at their own lives: many will look at themselves and see all their own unrealized aspirations. They may begin thinking about the ten pounds they never managed to lose, the businesses they never started, or the courses they never took. When they see you succeeding, they may feel envious or even inferior.

Accomplishing goals for yourself should never be about making others jealous, but some people will feel this way anyway. So many of us tell ourselves we "can't," because denial is easier than the real work of change. By your example, you will be showing others that their excuses—the lies they've been telling themselves for years—are false. You'll make them realize that their excuses keep them stuck in lives they don't love. And unfortunately, when this happens, these people might not want you around anymore; every time they see you, you will represent all the dreams they never followed through on. You will represent success. The success that empowers you to love your life.

Finding supportive people on your journey can be tough. When I was in some of my life's most transformational periods, I actually needed to break away from, or limit my time with, many of the people I used to rely on. Not because I was mad or disappointed, but because I needed to surround myself with those who were positive influences and further along on their own journeys than I was.

At the end of this chapter, you'll also find a list of various areas various in your life where you may need support. I learned this list from one of my mentors, Mark Cole, CEO of The John Maxwell Company.

As soon as you identify the areas in your life in which you need help, somehow the universe will bring that help. Seriously, it may sounds crazy, but as soon as I recognized that I needed some new people to help me in specific areas of my life, they started to appear.

When my life was under construction, one of my own

goals was self-employment, so I knew I needed a mentor/ coach who had experience with building a business. I sat down with a man named Clifton Maclin of the International Maxwell Certification Program. Clifton is a phenomenal man who has owned a successful business for over thirty years. He also served in the Vietnam War, has mentored the children of inmates, and has dedicated his life to service. I didn't know it then, but Clifton would become one of the most influential mentors in my life. His advice and guidance has helped my business grow and flourish. His belief in my skills as a speaker, author, and leadership trainer encouraged me to write this book.

One of my passions has always been leadership development; Clifton helped me to realize that certification through The John Maxwell Team was perfect for me. After being certified, I wanted to learn how to train others in leadership development; I reached out to a wonderful woman, Kellie George, who is another member of The John Maxwell Team. She's a great teacher, understands how to deliver content in a way that helps audiences learn, and she's passionate about sharing her expertise. Plus, Kellie turned out to be a great friend, which was a bonus since I was trying to find new positive people to surround myself with.

I encourage you to start thinking about the people you need in your life while it's under construction. Remember, just like you can't build a house by yourself, neither can you design a life by yourself. After you've targeted the areas in your life that need change, try asking yourself: Do I need a life- coach? A business mentor? A "thinking" partner to bounce ideas off of? An accountability partner to keep me on track? A really good friend who will simply support me? Each of us needs different types of support, so spend some time identifying your own needs. And it's okay to try things out—don't worry if you don't have all the support in place right away. When a path is right for you, these people will appear naturally as a part of your exploration process.

## Designing Your Life: Questions for Grow For Your Journey

When you are designing a life you love, you will need to change and grow. Change may not be easy, but by identifying key areas to focus on, your path will be intentioned and a bit easier.

1. These questions are taken from John Maxwell's book *The 15 Invaluable Laws of Growth*. Review these carefully. Put some time and effort into identifying who and what nurtures you personally.

- Music—What songs lift me?
- Thoughts—What ideas speak to me?
- Experiences—What experiences rejuvenate me?
- Friends—What people encourage me?
- Recreation—What activities revive me?
- Soul—What spiritual exercises strengthen me?
- Hopes—What dreams inspire me?
- Home—What family members care for me?
- Giftedness—What blessings activate me?
- Memories—What recollections make me smile?

- Books—What have I read that changed me?

2. Ask yourself: Am I in a growth environment or not? How can I set up a growth environment for myself? (Note: a growth environment can be literal or figurative, or both. I recommend making your home office or workspace a growth zone for you.)

3. What do I need to do right now to jumpstart my growth? Read a book? Attend an event? Listen to a leader? Do some research? Find some help?

4. If I could wave a magic wand and magically "fix" one area of my life, what would it be? Now, what do I need to do in reality to make this happen?

5. Think about some of the areas in your life where you may want to seek out mentors/friends for support. The list below comes from my mentor, Mark Cole:

- Relationship: Who can help me with my relationship?
- Parenting: Who can help me learn how to parent better?

- Personal Growth: Who can help me on my personal growth journey?
- Business/Career Goals: Who can help me grow my business or career?
- Physical Health: Who can help me be physically healthy?
- Financial Health: Who can help me get my financial life in order?
- Spirituality: Who can help me navigate my faith?

Examining yourself critically is an important step in your process. Congratulations on taking identifying the areas in which you most need growth!

# 5

*Collecting Ideas
for Your New Life*

"When I was five years old, my mother always told
me that happiness was the key to life. When I went to
school, they asked me what I wanted to be when I
grew up. I wrote down 'happy.' They told me I didn't
understand the assignment, and I told them they
didn't understand life." —John Lennon

I was a child when I first starting thinking about living a
life I could love as an adult. At eight years old, I would lie
in bed at night after my mom had tucked me in and I had
said my prayers. I would stare at the ceiling and imagine
myself as an adult. "How can I be happy?" I wondered.
Tons of questions would swirl in my mind: Where would
I live? Who would I marry? How many kids would I have?
What would I do in my career?

At eight years old, I didn't know much about life, but I did know that I wanted a life that was happy and full of many people to love. I wanted to be excited about the adventure each day would bring and be positively bursting with energy. I didn't know exactly what all that would look like, but I dreamed of it anyway. And, at eight years old, my dreams were *big*. I still had a childlike imagination at that age; I still had all the uninhibited creativity of a child!

As I grew older, my priorities and desires sharpened. I realized that I really, really, wanted to have my own family: a sweet, kind, loving husband; a few children; and a pet dog or two. I wanted a beautiful, spacious home in a safe, quiet neighborhood. I also became interested in starting my own business and gave some thought to my career.

That was my dream; your dream will be different. You are a unique person with your own roadmap, and your perfect life will be different from anyone else's. And that's okay. You don't want to be like anyone else. I'm sure you already have many ideas about what you want your own life to look like.

Here are some tips on collecting ideas for your own designed life.

### 1. Create an image board using Pinterest

Pinterest is my favorite site for designing and organizing my projects visually. Pinterest is a great way to collect beautiful pictures of what your designed life might look like and keep them all in one place. Start creating image boards related to various areas of your life—friends, fitness, home, business, play, travel, quotes, inspiration. You can have as many boards as you like, there's no limit. Once you've categorized your boards, you can start exploring. You can search the site for any sort of visual content you want, and you can "pin" interesting things to your boards. I love what comes up when I start searching on Pinterest; the images and ideas I find often get my creative juices flowing.

### 2. Begin journaling

Start writing down some of the things that you'd love to have in your life. Use any method of inspiration you can find, even the types that feel "weird." As odd as this may sound, one source of inspiration may be jealousy. Look at the people around you and find things that make you feel jealous. Not jealous in an obsessive or envious way, but in a way that makes you think, "Hey, I'd like that to be a part of my life someday." Write these in your journal. For example, when I was in elementary school, I had a friend whose family had a beautiful home and a solid business; they were able to dress well and travel often. I remember thinking, "I want that life when I'm an adult." As I grew, I used my friend's family as an example—they reminded me that creating a life like that for myself was a priority of mine. I wasn't envious of my friend—she was wonderful to me—but I knew that someday I wanted to be able to provide my family with the same things her family had.

A word of caution, however. Jealousy is a fine motivator; envy is not. Envy is destructive and self-consuming, and it will only make you feel sorry for yourself. Don't dwell on the things you don't have; focus instead on how setting goals will help you grow.

I would also set aside time to think and reflect before each writing session. Find a few moments wherever you can... like after you tuck your children into bed, or early in the morning before everyone else is awake. It doesn't really matter when you write, as long as you take time to do it. Thinking and reflecting are important parts of this process, too.

### 3. Energize yourself

We all have certain things that energize us and excite us, and we all have things that drain our energy. Make a list of the things that get you fired up in a good way—the things you love doing so much that you could do them every day without getting bored.

Some people describe these things as their passions. You may be like I was before I designed a life I could love; back then, I had taken so much of my life for granted for so long that I could barely remember my passions. If you're in a similar situation, that's okay. Don't worry too much, but do start thinking about the things you used to love to do. Drawing? Writing? Dancing? Yoga? Basketball? Reading? Recall the things that brought you joy, then write them all down.

I first learned about the VIA Survey, which I mentioned in Chapter One, from my chiropractor. (Note: You never know who exactly will help you along your journey. Start talking to people you trust and see what happens!) I must have mentioned to him that I was in the process of figuring out what energizes me, because he directed me to the test online. To help you with energizing yourself, I highly recommend you take the VIA test, because the VIA helps you to identify your own values; whenever you're stressed or drained you can review your values, which will help you get back on track.

When I took the VIA test, I had creativity as my

number one value, yet I hadn't really developed that part of myself in years. As a child, I would draw for hours and hours, design pretend homes, and dance and sing all the time. Yet as an adult, I had gradually stopped doing these things, because the adult world simply isn't as conducive to creativity. The VIA test also made me realize that I didn't have a single creative outlet in my adult life... NONE. I always felt drained of energy because I never took the time to fill myself back up with the things I valued and was good at.

After that realization, I started a blog about the building of our new home. I was able to design the blog, write it, and communicate creatively with others. I had started a blog just for my family and friends, yet it very quickly attracted thousands of visitors. (You can visit www.theliddlehouse.com to read it.) People got really into it... I was even stopped at a local Starbucks by a reader. When I began filling myself up with what I valued, I began affecting others positively as well. The same can happen for you.

### 4. Ask the $10 million question

One thing that may really help when your life is under construction is to start talking to others about the goals you want to achieve. Ask yourself: If I hit the lottery tomorrow for $10 million and never had to work again, what would I do?

- Where would I live?
- Would I want to work, and, if so, what would I do?
- Who would I help?

- Where would I travel?
- What wouldn't be important to me anymore?

The $10 million dollar question will help you get clarity on what you really want. So that you can talk about all these things clearly, take some time to write all your answers down. When we write, it helps with memory retention and things stick with us more easily. Our goals become more real to us, and therefore more likely to become a focal point when we interact with others.

5. Keep moving forward

You're on a roll now aren't you? Are ideas now flowing into your head? I hope so. This means that your ideal life is inside of you just waiting to escape. Capture it. Make it yours to live. Your life is precious. Make it the best and most amazing life that you can. Why not put your time and energy in creating a life you will absolutely love? Even if you can only move forward a little bit each day, keep going. A little work now will pay off when you begin experiencing your dream life. You can do it!

# Designing Your Life: Questions for Collecting Ideas for Your New Life

Dreaming about your awesome new life is the fun part. Now is the time to collect images and ideas that make your heart happy. The images represent the goals and dreams that until now only lived inside your own head. Take this time to think, reflect, and utilize your innate creative abilities.

1. Have I created a Pinterest board and started collecting ideas?

2. Did I start a journal and begin writing about what my life will look like? Who are the people that are a part of my new life? What kind of work will I be doing in this new life?

3. Did I take the VIA test? What did I discover? Were the results of this surprising to me? Why or why not? Did I learn anything about my values? Are there areas in my life where I could be integrating my values to help fill myself up when I'm feeling drained?

4. Review your answers from the $10 million lottery questions.

- Where would I live?
- Would I want to work, and, if so, what would I do?
- Who would I help?
- Where would I travel?
- What wouldn't be important to me anymore?

Taking the time to collect ideas about what your life will look like will help you design the life you want. Congratulations on putting together these valuable ideas!

A Quick Note:

You may or may not want material things in your life, and that's okay. There are many people doing meaningful, impactful work in some of the poorest countries of the world, and they are blessed beyond measure. I love to hear about those who are happy and fulfilled by this kind of work, and I hope someday to do some missionary work in a developing nation. One of my dreams is to accompany John Maxwell on a transformational leadership training retreat in a country with an emerging economy.

# 6

## *Detours on Your Journey*

"If you can't describe what you are doing as a process, you don't know what you're doing."

— W. Edwards Deming

My Grandfather, Paul Michels, Sr., was one of my greatest mentors. When I was fresh out of college, I would spend hours and hours with him each week. He was over eighty years old at that time and was generous with his wisdom. Whenever I'd tell him about an issue I was facing, Grandpa Michels used to look at me with his strikingly blue eyes and say, "Al, life is a process of ups and downs. You learn from both."

If I was having an "up" life moment, I would be okay with his advice. However, when I was in a "down" life moment, I'd become contemplative. I'd ask myself a whole slew of questions: How is life a process? What should I do now? How will I get through this situation? The questions would keep coming and my frustration would increase. In "down" life moments, I would be disappointed by my inability to control my life. I felt like a victim with no power; it was a terrible feeling of loneliness, dejection, sadness, and anger. Sometimes I would stay in a state of despair for days... or even weeks.

Only now, after designing my new life, do I realize just how right Grandpa Michels was. When your life is under construction, there will always be detours. That's okay as long as you learn from them. In fact, sometimes our detours are exactly the things that we need to be doing to prepare for the next stage—whatever the next stage may be. Even when you are unsure of why you're taking a detour at the time, eventually it will make sense.

One of my most difficult life moments came soon after college. I had just turned down an amazing job in my field at a company in Texas; this company was rated as one of "America's Best Places to Work," but I declined the position because wanted to stay in northern Wisconsin with my family. Beyond that, I was applying to local jobs every single day, yet I wasn't getting interviews. Money was increasingly tight; I needed an income to pay the bills. I felt lost and useless. I'd have lunch every day with one of my friends just to get out of the house, then cry all the way home. When had I graduated, I felt so sure my dream job would soon appear, but now I couldn't even find work in my field. I felt so desperate that I considered going back to the Texas company to see if they had another position available.

I began substitute teaching. I love children and I

appreciate teachers, but I learned that I didn't have the patience to teach every day, all day; this was not my life's path. But while I was teaching, I realized that I needed to take a major detour if I were going to be successful. I decided that if no one was going to hire me in my field, I would start my own business.

"Leap and the net will appear!" is an old saying, but it's exactly what happened when I started my marketing business at twenty-three years old. The following spring I was contacted by local realtors who engaged my services. I created an entire marketing campaign for their multi-million-dollar condo development. From there, my business kept growing. I had so much work that I could only keep up by working nights and weekends. It was exhilarating and exhausting. Soon, I was making more money than I would have if I had taken a full-time job, plus I loved having the freedom to make my own schedule. Okay, I won't lie, during those first few years I was working all the time. But that was alright—I was excited about supporting my clients; creating strategic marketing plans to meet their needs energized me.

A second detour on my journey came in 2008, although this one truly wasn't planned. That autumn, the real estate bubble burst and my clients no longer had the funds to pay for my services. I needed to find a job quickly.

Although it was outside of my field, I took a job as the director of the Great Start Collaborative, a non-profit that serves schools in Michigan's Upper Peninsula. I was in charge of building a volunteer board of twenty non-profit professionals who were to revamp and implement early childhood learning systems. The school was an hour and a half away from my home, but I managed the commute... even in the snowy winter. Advocacy was a big part of the job, too, and I traveled all over Michigan, plus attended many meetings in Lansing, which was ten hours away.

Although this job wasn't in my field, I learned a lot from my detour, and the position turned out to be one of the best leadership learning experiences of my career. I struggled a little bit at the beginning, but I was driven by the desire to improve the lives of some of Michigan's poorest, most rural children. When I first took the job, I was intimated at the prospect of leading people who were twice my age. I knew I needed help, and that's when John Maxwell's Maximum Impact Mentoring program appeared in my life, almost as if by magic. Sometimes, when you ask the universe for something, the universe gives it to you, no questions asked.

The desire to become a better advocate for these children put me on my own path to personal leadership. I learned a lot from John Maxwell's CDs, books, and materials, and I used his leadership strategies to reach politicians on both the city and state levels. I became an advocate for children and their families. It was such an impactful experience, and I feel blessed to have had the opportunity.

This detour was priceless. Now when I look back at the past decade of my life, I can see that much of my professional growth has happened because of the things I learned from those who were leaders in their fields. I studied successful people and started implementing the concepts and techniques they were teaching me. I don't think I ever would have learned these lessons if I hadn't found myself in a position where I needed guidance.

Detours are learning experiences, even when they are a struggle. I find that my lowest or most challenging moments—the times when I feel terrible or the most unsure—are also the moments when I learn the most about myself. These moments have challenged me to keep a positive attitude despite my current reality; they've taught me how to believe in myself, and they helped me build and cultivate relationships. In my low moments, I've learned how to ask for help; I've figured out that surrounding myself with intelligent, happy, and kind people is essential to my well-being; and most of all, I've learned that I need to be challenged and have a sense of purpose in all that I do. I use these lessons every day to push myself further so that I can fill myself up with the things that make me happy.

My detour to Michigan—along with the birth of Avery and the craziness of moving and building a new home—put me on my path to my true vocation. In the midst of all of this chaos, I was still searching for my own fulfillment and purpose; I would not let the busyness of my everyday life overwhelm my search for my purpose. I searched and searched and prayed and prayed. And one day I figured out what I needed: I signed up for The John Maxwell Team.

John Maxwell had established The John Maxwell Team to train others about leadership and personal development. From day one, I was hooked—I had found my "thing." I started to dive into The John Maxwell Team's online courses. Even with my life swirling in a hundred different directions, I'd push myself to find the time to devote to the courses. I'm sure many around me were wondering why I was adding leadership training to everything else on my plate, but, personally, I feel that when an opportunity presents itself, you don't wait. You just do it. You make the time. You find the resources. You make it happen.

Especially when you're trying to grow yourself personally or professionally, you may find that life gets more difficult before it gets better. The added complication may or may not be the result of a detour, but in all cases, truly transformational change requires a serious commitment and effort. You are trying to remake yourself into someone different, a better version of yourself, and it's okay if things get hard or if you don't feel you have as much support from friends and family as you used to. Your journey is a personal journey. Try to find the lessons at every stage, especially from your detours. Be patient with yourself as you grow and change.

## Designing Your Life: Questions for Detours on Your Journey

When has life taken you on a detour? Remember to acknowledge that learning often comes from some of our most difficult struggles. When your detour comes to an end, you will emerge stronger, more courageous, and have more to give others. These questions will help you reflect on your detours.

1. What have been the detours in my life?

2. Look back at the timeline you created of your life. Ask yourself: How did I feel at each stage?

Excited, scared, fearful? Which of these events were the most important to my growth?

3. Are you feeling alone or unsupported in your growth journey? Take a few minutes to write out some of the areas where you feel unsupported or frustrated. Sometimes things have to get harder before they get better, but remember it will all be okay in the end.

4. What are some of the ups and downs I have experienced? What have they taught me about myself? How can I use these experiences to help me design a life I can love?

5. How do I want to transform my own life? Are there specific areas in life where I need change and transformation?

Planned or unplanned, detours are learning experiences. Congratulations on opening yourself up to detours!

# 7

## *Your Negative Voice and Your Laughing Voice*

"You need to learn how to select your thoughts just the same way you select your clothes every day. This is a power you can cultivate. If you want to control things in your life so bad, work on the mind. That's the only thing you should be trying to control."
—Elizabeth Gilbert

You really do want to design a life you will love. You're now fully invested and ready for change. Yet, whenever you take steps toward that change, there's a little voice in your head giving you pause. That's the voice of negativity and self-doubt, which threatens to derail anyone who is designing a life they will love. So many hear this voice and just give up; self-doubt tells them their ideas are dumb and that they don't deserve a new life. But you're different. You've resolved to change, and this book will equip you with an awareness of self-doubt and the ability to tell that voice to *shut up*. By simply understanding that negativity and self-doubt are a part of the process, you'll be able to achieve more than you ever thought possible.

I worked my way through college as a waitress at a high-end steak house. On my first day, I shadowed a senior waitress. She walked me through the restaurant's system of waiting on tables: there were procedures to follow for everything from greeting the patrons to delivering the check. As the senior waitress worked, I asked her questions when necessary, and I took notes for my own use so that I'd remember how I was supposed to do things.

The waitress who trained me was one of the most encouraging and bubbly people I've ever met. She smiled at the patrons and seemed to enjoy serving them. After I had waited on my first table, she pointed out everything I did right while minimizing what I did wrong.

This waitress had a "laughing voice" and she exemplified a positive encourager. Even now, years later, whenever I stop by the steak house, she remembers me. She smiles and says how glad she is to see me. She asks about my family. When I leave the restaurant, I feel happy and encouraged. Her laughing voice is always filled with optimism, positive thoughts, and abundance thinking.

Your own laughing voice is what you need to train yourself to use in your thoughts. I know that might sound weird, but as you practice, your own laughing voice will emerge. However, to fully access your laughing voice, you will first need to recognize that other voice inside of you, your "negative voice."

Your negative voice is the voice of self-doubt. We all hear it sometimes; it criticizes everything. It is the part of ourselves that is fearful of change. When we listen to our negative voice, we get caught in a quicksand of excuses—"I can't," or "That will never happen for me," or "It's too hard."

I have a friend who is very analytical and very negative. He likes finding problems and pointing them out. He watches the news constantly, reads the paper daily, and enjoys lamenting about all the bad stuff going on in the world. He never seems to have control over anything in his life, and his days are filled with reactionary behavior. If he sees something on the news that angers him, he reacts; if he gets a phone call that upsets him, he reacts; if he feels someone was rude to him, he reacts. Even worse, he seems to glee in minimizing others. His days are filled with depression, stress, and low energy. He can even turn positive news into something bad—he'll ignore the good altogether because no one should have anything good in their life since he can't have goodness in his.

It's sad to say, but I don't think anything positive will ever happen in this friend's life. His priorities are all over the place, and low self-confidence oozes out of him like a sickness. He's fearful of change and wants his world to remain exactly the same forever. When things inevitably do change, he has a difficult time adapting. On top of all of this, my friend also has a scarcity mind-set, so there is never, ever enough of anything. He thinks he needs to tear down others in order to have enough for himself. In business, he obsesses about his competition. In his personal life, he rarely spends quality time with his friends and family.

Whenever I speak with this friend, I feel discouraged,

drained, and hopeless, and my own negative voice resurfaces: I have to fight it back. You must do the same with your own inner negative voice. If you let the negative voice rule your thoughts, it will sabotage all your great ideas and will talk you out of your aspirations. If you listen to this voice, you will never be good enough, you'll never have enough, you'll never measure up. This voice will taint your outlook with a very negative, overly critical eye, and make you second-guess yourself and your accomplishments.

Your negative voice is toxic to you and your growth. It may seem extreme to say that just a few negative thoughts can have a profound impact on you, but it's true. You need to guard yourself from your negative voice when you are trying to grow and change.

Especially in the beginning phases of self-growth, you will be a bit unsure of yourself. Everything you're doing will be new. This phase is similar to when you first learned to ride a bike. You were probably very excited about your new bike, but when you first tried to ride it, you felt disoriented and unstable. That's exactly how it feels when you first start designing a life you love.

Your new life will seem exciting at first, but then the real work of stretching beyond your comfort zone begins—and that's a little scary. Day after day, you will invest more and more energy into designing your new life, yet it may take a while before you see any kind of results. However, just like when you were learning to ride your bike, you will be hopeful that—with patience and practice—you'll soon have a whole new type of freedom.

Don't be discouraged if the journey to your new life takes longer than you anticipated. In an ideal world, results would require little effort and be almost immediate, but that's not how it works in reality. In our current fast-paced, hyper-connected, Internet-enabled world, it's easy to forget that real goals require real effort, and real effort takes real time. If you are seriously designing your life, the process will be as much about the journey as the destination. As John Maxwell says, "Anything worthwhile is uphill."

You can, and will, succeed in designing your life. One of the biggest hurdles that you need to overcome is your own negative voice—banish it so that your personal laughing voice can emerge.

Here are some quick ways to kick your negative voice out of your head:

1. Stop, or strictly limit, watching the news. We all need, to some extent, to know what's going on in the world around us, but limit your news-watching to only one day a week—or watch only if something really important happens—and this includes time on internet news sites. Too much news only fills your mind with negativity.

2. Identify when your negative voice is most likely to creep into your head. For example, if you are prone to having negative thoughts at bedtime, try creating a relaxing bedtime routine that will help you get to sleep. If you're less stressed, it will be easier to recognize and dismiss your negative voice.

3. Find someone close to you who will support you in kicking your negative voice out of your thoughts. Explain what your negative voice is, and ask your friend to gently point out when your words or actions are demonstrating negativity. The key to this is asking for help from someone nonjudgmental who truly loves and supports you. Be sure not to get defensive when you're told your negative voice is speaking. Instead, stop, make a note, and change the subject.

4. Be patient and kind with yourself. Everyone is so hard on themselves these days! We all make mistakes when trying something new; learning takes time. No one hits a home run their first time at bat, so don't worry about it. If your negative voice slips into your thoughts or words, kindly say to yourself, "Negative voice, I don't listen to you anymore." That's it. Don't beat yourself up over it.

5. Exercising: This is one of the quickest ways to kick your negative voice out of your thoughts. Walking, running, bike riding, kickboxing, dancing, swimming... whatever type of exercise suits you best, go ahead and do it. Exercise is the body's natural way of energizing, and we release

endorphins (chemicals that make us feel good) when we work up a sweat. Exercise regularly and you'll notice that your negative voice is quiet during your workouts.

Once you've gotten pretty good at kicking your negative voice out of your head, it's time to find your laughing voice. Welcoming your personal laughing voice involves intentionally filling your mind and your life with positive energy. This takes time and focus. You are exploring the space inside yourself where you feel the most drained, negative, or empty; you must be very mindful about what you choose to fill yourself back up with. If you aren't careful, your negative voice will creep back in.

Here are some steps to help welcome your laughing voice:

1. Be more present: Many times, our lives are so filled with busyness that we're either thinking about what happened yesterday or are anticipating what might happen tomorrow. Whether your mind moves into the past or the future, the underlying result is the same: you're distracted from the here and now. In order to be more positive, you need to be more present in your life. That means focusing on where you are right now, today, in this moment. You can't undo the past, nor do you need to obsess about the

future. Be present. If you do this, your laughing voice will be more available to you.

2. Find your happy place: You've probably heard this before, but did you take this very good advice? If so, where is your happy place? If not, your happy place can be found by reflecting on your life: When are you at your absolute best? When do you feel the most energy? Is there a time of day when you are able to accomplish the most? To find, or revisit, your happy place, you must be intentional about identifying where your own most positive energy naturally lives. Harness it.

3. Choose the right attitude: We all have days when nothing seems to go right, but you can choose how you react to stress. You can be miserable and self-pitying, or you can choose to laugh at all your bad luck while reminding yourself that tomorrow will be better. For example, one day my child literally puked all over me during a doctor's visit. I was covered in vomit—I had puke running down the front of me, it even dripped onto my shoes! It was gross, and I could have let it ruin my whole day. But instead, I chose to laugh about it; I called my husband and said, "I win today for being the best mom ever." You *choose* your attitude each day, why not make it a good one?

4. Self-Affirmations: When we take the time to state our intentions and verbalize positive thoughts, it can be transformative. Okay, I'll admit it... I thought self-affirmations were bogus until I tried them for myself. I used positive affirmations to lose sixty pounds after I had my second child! I purposefully began talking to myself in a more positive, goal-oriented language. Instead of saying, "I'm going to try to work out," I said, "I work out four times each week." Instead of saying, "I want to eat healthier," I told myself, "I make healthy food choices and I don't drink my calories," and reminded myself how much better I feel when I do this. By demanding the best from myself, I grew into a better version of myself. I reached my goal weight without ever looking at the scale. If positive affirmations can help me with my goals, they can help you with yours, too.

5. Love yourself: Do you wake up each morning and tell yourself how much you love yourself? We need to fill ourselves up with whatever we want to give to the world, and this includes love. If we fill ourselves with love, then we will be able to give more love to those around us. Practice loving yourself. This is not selfish or vain, it's a part of self-care. When you look in the mirror, appreciate everything about yourself, even those so-called flaws. Take care of yourself: there's only

one you on the entire planet. You are here for a purpose and we need you. Love yourself wholly and completely, then start sending all that love out into the world. You are worth it!

We all have positive and negative thought-voices within us. Doesn't that make you feel a bit more normal? The choice that we have to make is deciding which voice to listen to. Successful people choose to listen to their laughing voice on a daily basis: unsuccessful people listen to their negative voice. Listen only to your very best self!

## Designing Your Life: Questions for Your Negative Voice and Your Laughing Voice

Which voice do you regularly listen to? Take this quiz to find out, and don't forget to tally up your points at the end. If you answer *yes* to a question, give yourself the points indicated in parenthesis; if you answer *no*, don't give yourself any points.

1. Do I watch the news or read the newspaper for more than a few moments each day? (-1 pt)
2. Do people often tell me I have a negative attitude? (-1 pt)
3. Do I tend to look at the bright side of life? (+3 pts)
4. Do I live in the present? Am I focused on what I can control today? (+3 pts)
5. Do I care for myself physically, emotionally, and spiritually? (+3 pts)

6. Do I focus on things that are out of my control? (-1 pt)
7. Do I smile and laugh almost every day? (+3 pts)
8. Do I have a positive attitude? (+3 pts)
9. Have I identified my happy place? (+3 pts)
10. Do I feel stress, worry, or anxiety often? (-1 pt)

Score:

- -4 to 1: You are letting your negative voice fill your head! Look for ways of reducing your negativity.
- 3 to 8: You oscillate between your laughing voice and your negative voice. Take time to identify when each voice is dominant. Try to replace your negative voice as often as you can.
- 9 to 18: You are listening to your laughing voice every day! You use positive self-talk to approach your life.

Changing the way we think and speak to ourselves takes work, and may even feel uncomfortable. Congratulations on standing up to your negative voice and welcoming your laughing voice!

# 8

# *Use Your Imagination to Dream Bigger*

**"Logic will get you from *A* to *B*. Imagination will take you everywhere."** —Albert Einstein

My five-year-old son Logan uses his imagination all day long. From the time he wakes up until the time he goes to sleep, he is pretending and playing. He goes from being Batman and asking me to pretend I'm the Joker, to becoming an engineer and building a "ginormous" structure out of LEGOs. Sometimes he runs in circles making engine sounds. When my husband asks what he's doing, Logan explains, "Dad, I'm a race car and that's my engine. I need more gas." ("Gas" generally means he wants a snack for "fuel.") I appreciate my son's innate ability to use his imagination.

Somewhere between childhood and adulthood, our innate ability to use our imagination leaves us. Or perhaps it doesn't quite leave us, perhaps it's more like a muscle that atrophies from underuse. I'm going to suggest that you start using your imagination muscle regularly to strengthen it again.

*The Magic of Thinking Big* by David J. Schwartz, Ph.D. is one of my favorite books about dreaming, thinking bigger, and using your imagination. In *The Magic of Thinking Big*, Schwartz identifies six crucial tools for thinking more creatively: believing it can be done; being receptive to new ideas and experimentation; asking yourself how to do better; asking yourself how you can do more; adopting "listening and accepting" as a practice; and stretching your mind by associating with new people.

**Tool One: Believing it can be done.**

When you start to change your perspectives, you may—almost as if by magic—develop new ideas that could contain the solution to any given problem you are facing. As Schwartz explains, "When you believe, your mind finds ways to do." Believing that you can and will design a life you love is the key ingredient for your journey.

**Tool Two: Being receptive to new ideas and experimentation.**

Oftentimes in life, we can get set in our ways or bound by traditional thinking. The only way to break this habit is to start experimenting. By trying out new things and becoming more accepting of new ideas, you will start to have new thoughts. As you have more and more new thoughts, you'll start to wonder why you never tried something you've always been interested in, or why you haven't challenged yourself in a certain area. This is your imagination at work.

### Tool Three: Asking yourself to do better.

Grow your capacity by asking yourself, in Schwartz's words, "How can I do better?" The best part of self-growth is that there's no limit on potential! When your life is under construction, you can do and achieve anything and everything you set your mind to. So, by asking yourself, "How can I do better?" you are setting yourself up for continual self-improvement and growth.

### Tool Four: Asking yourself to do more.

Schwartz tells us to ask, "How can I do more?" and explains that "capacity is indeed a state of mind." Reflect for a moment: how much could you achieve if you really started to push yourself and truly believed that, yes, you *can*? I would suggest that you devote several brainstorming sessions to exploring how you can do more with the time and resources you currently have. You may be surprised to learn that you've been missing something obvious, or that you have someone in your support network who could help you in a new way.

### Tool Five: Practicing "asking and listening."

"Ask and listen and you'll obtain raw material for reaching sound decisions," explains Schwartz. None of us know everything; we need to learn from each other. This must be a conscious effort on your part—people who are trying to grow themselves seek out others to learn from. Those who are committed to self-growth actively listen, ask great questions, and use others' feedback to modify their own behavior. In effect, they are absorbing the wisdom of other people and therefore becoming wiser themselves.

When your life is under construction, you will need to ask great questions, actively seek help, and listen. This will help you reflect on your own goals and help you recognize what you need to modify most in your life. But don't stop there. There's a critical next step, too. Go back to the people who advised you, thank them, and then tell them how you implemented their advice. More than likely, these people will have other thoughts to share. This is how you create mentors who can help you navigate the new life you are designing.

Tool Six: Stretching your mind by meeting new people.

In order to grow yourself, you need to start associating with new people, people who are outside of your normal sphere. This is critical to your becoming the person that you want to become. When my life was under construction, I knew I needed to find some new peers—people who weren't currently in my life. For me, I needed to surround myself with positive, like-minded people. I found my new positive people at a local mastermind group, which is type of peer-to-peer mentoring system. Before each monthly meeting, I would get giddy thinking about who I would meet and what I would learn. I'd leave each meeting fired up and ready to continue on my self-discovery process. Eventually, I began helping to coordinate these meetings; I felt honored to be able to help other people find the positive-growth environments they needed. What an amazing feeling!

These six tools are crucial to using your imagination and dreaming bigger! Remember to start small—don't try to use all of these tools at once or else you might overwhelm yourself. But, if one tool resonates with you more than the others, perhaps you should try that one first. Go out into the world and find opportunities to use your favorite tool.

§

Back when I was in college, I got a funny card from my mom with a dog on it that said, "There's not a shred of evidence that life has to be serious." And it's true. As adults, we become so utterly serious about everything. We stop appreciating all of the amazing things around us, and instead start focusing on stuff like the paying the bills. We all have to pay bills, of course, but we can decide how much energy and time we are willing to devote to these mundane necessities. When we reduce the mundanity in our lives, it frees up space for creativity and imagination.

Personally, I hate paying bills. I refuse to spend even one more precious minute than is absolutely necessary on the monthly finances. When I decided bill-paying was something that was guzzling too much of my time, I set up automatic bill-pay for most of my bills. Now it takes me a few minutes each month to pay the bills, rather than hours. Even better is that I don't have to waste precious time worrying about deadlines and due dates because payments are automatic.

My point is that we need to stop filling our time with—and expending our energy on—things that don't bring us happiness. Identify those boring, but necessary, things that you loathe doing the most, then figure out a way to A) stop doing them, B) reduce the time it takes to do them, or C) pay someone else to do them for you. It's really that simple. If you hate cleaning your house, hire a cleaner. If paying for this for extra expense gives you pause, skip eating out a couple times a week or find other ways to tighten your belt. If you don't want to mow the lawn, hire the kid down the street—she'll probably be eager for the chance to earn some money.

Start being strategic about the mundane things you will allow yourself to do. If there's something you truly hate doing, STOP. Life is too short to fill our days with things that make us miserable, especially when we could be focusing our time and our energy on doing the things we love.

Take a little bit of time to think about all of those things that are eating up your time and sapping your energy. Make a list. Ask yourself: how can I stop doing these things? Of course, there will always be a few things on the list that you—and only you—must take care of, but if you look at your list with a strategic, mindful eye, I bet you can find three things you can let go or minimize for every one thing you absolutely MUST do.

After you've found ways of reducing energy-sapping mundanity, it's time to let your imagination fly. Using your imagination is a skill that you have deep inside of you, even if you've forgotten it's there. Using your imagination will help you see your world beyond your current constraints. When you "think bigger" and imagine what your life could be like, you can start moving in a different direction.

Walt Disney once said, "Every child is born blessed with a vivid imagination. But just as a muscle grows flabby with disuse, so the bright imagination of a child pales in later years if he ceases to exercise it." Disney was right, and

I bet he understood this from his own life experiences—he "failed forward" by being unsuccessful in any number of mundane jobs. Yet, Walt Disney proved himself to be one of the most imaginative men of the twentieth century: he created an entire magical world for children purely from his imagination.

Not everyone can be as imaginative as Disney, but that's okay. All you have to do is start small and imagine what your life could look like: your life needs to be filled with the people, experiences, and things that matter most to you. Everyone has a different picture of their ideal life—create your own world.

## Designing Your Life: Questions for Use Your Imagination to Dream Bigger

Your life is special. Take the time to reduce the clutter in your life and use your imagination. This is the time for you to dream big. Set your inhibitions aside while to do this exercise.

1. What would be the most amazing career I could ever have?


2. Where would be my most awesome place to live?

3. How would I look, or act, or dress if I were the best version of myself?

4. How can I help others?

5. How can I do more?

6. How can I do better?

7. Am I good listener? How can I improve my listening skills in order to learn from wise people?

8. Who do I need in my life to help stretch my mind?

9. What could I do that would fill me up?

Congratulations on stretching your thinking and using your imagination!

# 9

Become a
*Goal-Setting Pro*

"There are many things that will catch my eye, but
there are only a few things that will catch my heart."

—Tim Redmond

When you're designing a life you will love, you will have
a particular plan in mind about what your life should look
like. You may have a new career mapped out. You may
have plans for your family as a whole, or plans for yourself
personally. This is good. But then you come up with a goal
that doesn't fit into any of your plans. The goal is a brand-
new idea that excites and energizes you. Every time you
think about it, a smile spreads across your face, yet this
goal *really* doesn't fit in with the rest of your plans. Now
what?

Here are your options. You could just ignore that amazing, wonderful goal because it doesn't fit into your plans, or you could keep the goal and modify your plans. It's one or the other; I recommend the latter.

When I signed up for The John Maxwell Team with the goal of becoming a Certified Team Member, it was just after I'd given birth to Avery, moved to our new city, began building our new home, and—on top of all that—less than month after, I'd learned that my mom had been diagnosed with breast cancer. Life was swirling all around me and getting in the way of my new goal. Yet every time I thought about becoming certified, I would almost have to pinch myself... I was so excited that this opportunity had become available to me. Yet my life in that moment was not conducive to this new goal. Actually, it seemed like the world was conspiring against my new goal.

What could I do? I quit my training. I thought, "This is not the right time." Little did I know that it was the absolutely perfect time. God was at work. I called one of my friends and asked her what she thought I should do. She asked, "Allison, do you think you *need* this in your life right now? Does it make you happy? Excite you? Make you hopeful?" I was nodding on the other end of the phone as she was speaking to me. "Yes, all of those," I replied. "Then do it," she said.

I signed up for The John Maxwell Team again: it was one of the best life decisions I've ever made. I now had access to positive, wonderful, kind, like-minded individuals from all over the world. These people encouraged me. They helped me with my goals and were patient with my struggles. I was certified by The John Maxwell Team in March 2016. I felt so proud of myself for accomplishing an amazing goal even when life got in the way.

§

Many people think of goals as complicated and daunting, yet there's nothing complicated about them at all. A goal is simply something you're trying to do or want to achieve. There's no magic or mystery to it at all.

I recently was asked to speak to a group of professionals about setting goals. A few months after I gave the presentation, my friend came up to me and told me she had achieved the goal she had set for herself during the presentation. My friend's goal was to find a position in marketing, and she had implemented some of the techniques I'd spoken about. By using these techniques to foster her own success, she had managed to attract the interest of a great company. She was still in awe that she had landed the job of her dreams.

Stories like this make me smile. I was so incredibly happy for this friend because she is a talented, motivated person who deserves a position that will stretch her professionally. I feel fulfilled by having had a small hand in her success. I'm not taking credit for her good fortune—she's spent years and years developing herself professionally—but it's deeply satisfying to know that I was able to share techniques that helped her on her path to success.

There are many reasons to set goals. They can help us move forward in a specific direction, and they can help keep us focused. Goals remind us of what we want to achieve and help us think about the steps needed to get there. For these reasons and many more, I always recommend during my presentations that participants write their goals down.

The one thread that every true goal shares is an emotional connection. Your goal must be linked to something that's important to you. After all, if you don't have an emotional connection to a goal, it will be difficult for you to keep working toward it. When I lead my presentations, I encourage participants to think carefully about the emotional connections they have to their goals. I also recommend that they take the time to examine the emotions surrounding any given goal, as well as examine the impact those emotions have.

Recently, my friend Libby started to train for a half-marathon. She hadn't ever run a half-marathon before and wasn't in shape for such a long race. (A half-marathon is equal to just over thirteen miles.) Nevertheless, she had the goal of running the race anyhow. In her heart, she knew that accomplishing her goal would bring her confidence and fulfillment: this, I believe, was her true motivation.

Libby needed to be in peak physical shape for the race, so she researched training programs and then started following them. She began lifting weights to make her muscles stronger. And, of course, she started running a lot. By race day, she was prepared.

Libby ran the entire half-marathon and achieved her goal. When I saw her after the race, I knew she'd become a different person, both physically and emotionally. Not only was her physique lean and muscular, but she also exuded self-confidence. Libby achieved her goal, but the goal itself wasn't her real purpose. The purpose was to transform herself into a healthier, more confident version of herself. I was so proud of her.

As you design your life, you must craft your goals carefully. Another of my mentors, Paul Martinelli,

President of the John Maxwell Team, has taught me some of the most common mistakes we can make when setting up our goals. In his presentation, *The 5 Mistakes of Goal Setting*, Paul defines the five biggest goal-setting mistakes as: setting goals we know we can achieve; setting goals based on fixed plans; believing a goal isn't "real" if we don't know exactly how to achieve it; questioning the right to "do," "be," or "have" what we want; and thinking that a goal's true purpose is reaching the goal itself. He has given me permission to share them with you.

Mistake 1: Setting goals we know we can achieve.

When setting goals, sometimes you might think, "I'm pretty sure that I could do this because I did something similar last year." This isn't setting a true goal; it's using what you already know you can accomplish as a baseline for future achievement. The problem with this type of thinking is that it really limits your ability to push yourself out of your comfort zone. Goals are meant to be big. So big that when you achieve a goal, you stop and think, "Wow, I did that." Don't limit yourself by comparing your potential accomplishments to what you've done in the past. It won't work and it will limit you.

Instead, you should choose goals that are not attainable in your mind right now but would be absolutely amazing to achieve. Think of something that you've always wanted to do, but that your negative voice said you couldn't. Now ignore that voice and write the goal down. It's that simple.

Mistake 2: Setting goals based on a fixed plan.

At my previous job, we had to create strategic plans for everything. Our goals not only had to be tangibly measurable, but also had to fit inside preexisting plans. We might have had a wonderful and amazing idea for a goal, but if the idea didn't fit into the original plan, it got thrown out. I bet we lost many great ideas and goals just because they didn't fit our current plan. What a shame!

Don't worry about pre-set plans when setting your goals. If a great goal pops into your head but it doesn't fit your current plans, write it down anyway. Allow for possibility to arise when setting goals.

**Mistake 3: Believing a goal isn't "real" if we don't know exactly how to achieve it.**

It would be nice if all our goals came with a roadmap. It's common to want absolute clarity about how to achieve a goal before attempting it. But goals don't work like this. In fact, not being sure of how to reach your goal is sometimes an important part of the achievement process.

In order for you to become more than you are right now, you need to choose goals that push you outside of your comfort zone. That means that you won't be one hundred percent comfortable with your goal and you'll be working outside of your area of expertise. That's okay. You don't need to know how to accomplish something for it to be a goal—you'll figure it out along the way.

**Mistake 4: Questioning the right to "do," "be," or "have" what we want.**

As you start setting goals, you may start thinking to yourself, "I don't deserve that," or "I'm just not..." or "I can't..." If you find yourself thinking negative thoughts like these, *stop it!* This is self-sabotage. We are all human beings: there is no such thing as "less than" someone else, and no one inherently "deserves" any more than you do. If you want something, go for it. Why couldn't you be, have, or become exactly who or what you want? Don't let your negative voices creep into your head. Your life should be amazing, and there is enough for everyone. You don't need to compare yourself to anyone else. This is your life. You are designing it the exact way that you want it to turn out. Set your goal and tell yourself, "Yes I deserve this. I can make my life exactly what I want it to be."

Mistake 5: Thinking the purpose of a goal is reaching the goal itself.

This is my favorite myth. Goals are important, yes, but achieving them isn't the true purpose behind them. Achieving goals takes preparation, time, effort—a real investment of many different resources. Yet when you reach your goal, you'll realize that something greater has been happening all along, something behind the scenes. While you were sacrificing your time and energy, this *thing* happened inside you, and it transformed you: you became the person who just achieved the goal.

The purpose of a goal isn't merely to reach the goal—it's much more than that. The purpose is to become someone who can *achieve*. To achieve your goal, you had to grow and change: this is a goal's true purpose.

You must commit to becoming a goal-setting pro in order to design a life you will love. Setting goals is a critical part of your successful journey because goals help us pinpoint specific things we want or need in our lives. As Norman Vincent Peale, the author of *The Power of Positive Thinking*, once said, "All successful people have a goal. No one can get anywhere unless he knows where he wants to go and what he wants to be or do."

# Designing Your Life: Questions for Becoming a Goal-Setting Pro

Now that you know about the benefits of setting goals and have some information about avoiding common goal-setting mistakes, you can start writing down your own goals. I bet you'll be amazed by the results! You can also visit www.allisonliddle.com to download a goal-setting template.

Here are some great questions to answer when you are trying to come up with your goals.

1.  Where would I love to be thirty days [or sixty days, or six months, or one year] from now?

2.  Have I discovered any new opportunities on my journey that excite and inspire me?

3.  What could I do today that would be outside of my comfort zone?

4.  What is one area in my life where I have the greatest need right now for a goal? (personally, professionally, health, relationships, family, etc.)

5. Why is the goal in Number Four important to me?

6. What assumptions or "what ifs" are getting in the way of my goal?

7. What are some of my frustrations from my past and how do they apply to today?

8. What type of self-affirmations should I use to help boost my confidence and keep me focused on my goal?

9. What are my strengths? My talents? My abilities? My resources? My significance? My influence? (Idea: if you haven't already, take a personality profile test like the StrengthsFinder 2.0 to help you find the answers to these questions.)

10. What other ideas or thoughts do I have about my goals?

You did it. You started to think about your goals in

a tangible way. Congratulations on moving closer to achieving your goals!

# 10

The Day You Want
to Give Up

"Try not to resist the changes that come your way.
Instead, let life live through you. And do not worry
that your life is turning upside down. How do you
know that the side you are used to is better than the
side to come?" —Rumi

At this point on your journey, you are probably
somewhere in between designing your life and having a
life that's actively under construction. When your life is
under construction, you will inevitably have those days
where—no matter how hard you try—you just want to
give up.

Today I want to throw in the towel and give up. Things
in my life are utter in upheaval. There are about a dozen
people working to put the finishing touches on our new

home, and we move in TOMORROW! The renovations on our office are crazy, too; there are another three people working on that right now. When I stopped by the construction sites, I was asked so many questions that my head started to spin. Tomorrow we have movers coming to our rental home at 7:00 a.m., yet right now, in the new house, it doesn't look like there's enough room to put all our stuff; the new house is still full of power tools, building supplies, and workers. I just texted our builder to make sure it's okay for us to begin moving in, but who knows? There's still a huge pile of dirt on our new front lawn, and there's a bright green portable latrine in our driveway. We're having sixty guests coming on Saturday, but the carpet isn't installed correctly, there are still holes in our walls, and there's painting that needs to be touched up. Even the siding on the house isn't finished. It just doesn't seem like it will all be ready by Saturday, it really doesn't.

I wrote the above paragraph on the day I wanted to give up. I've included it here because I wanted to share the feeling of being overwhelmed with all of you, so that you know we all have "giving up" moments. After the day from hell, I went to Starbucks and treated myself to a chocolate chip cookie and some hot peach tea, and started writing in my journal.

When your life is under construction, you are going to have days when the world seems to be pushing your last button. You're going to want to yell, scream, cry, or—if you're like me—hide. And that's okay. It's healthy to recognize when you're feeling overwhelmed. When all that's happening around you simply seems like too much to handle, give yourself permission to take a cookie break. Everything will work out. It's okay if everything's not perfect. That doesn't mean you can't celebrate accomplishments so far.

And breathe. Let all of your worries melt away for a moment. Most of the things that feel really big right now are really just petty annoyances that won't matter a year from now. Everything will get done. Joel Osteen, a prominent minister, recommends that you categorize your problems into five-minute, five-hour, and five-month problems. By recognizing how big of an issue a problem really is, you'll be better equipped to deal with it.

One thing that I recently learned from John Maxwell is that there are many different answers to any challenge. Before I learned this, I would try my first possible solution to a problem; if my solution didn't work, I would think I had failed. But that's not true at all. There may be many different approaches to a given challenge, and any number of solutions. This is such a profound concept that I've been using it every day—especially when I was in the middle of two construction projects.

"When someone has been given much, much will be required in return; and when someone has been entrusted with much, even more will be required."
—Luke 12:48

I did have some rough days when I was writing this book. On one of these days, I spoke with my mentor Clifton Maclin. I told him how I truly felt: there are times when I feel I just can't go any further and I want to give up. Clifton is such an amazing, accomplished man who has done so many wonderfully amazing things that I'd have to write a full book to tell you all of them. He is a true servant-leader and I feel beyond blessed to call him my mentor. From a young age, Clifton has always had the mindset of a champion.

When I wanted to give up, Clifton's advice was so invaluable to me that I asked if I could share his story, *Never Give Up!*, with all of you:

When asked the question about whether I have ever wanted to "give up," I can say that "giving up" is virtually a foreign concept for me. I became clear about never giving up or quitting the pursuit of my goals when I was five years old. My mind-set was established that I could accomplish anything "humanly possible" if I was "absolutely determined" and clear about my goals, committed to doing whatever was necessary to train my mind, my emotions, and my body to "get the job done."

The particular incident that led to this understanding occurred because I was given a disassembled plastic replica 45 cal. automatic pistol as a Christmas present. The challenging part of assembling the pistol was the trigger mechanism. The pistol parts were tooled to fit together without glue or screws, just like a real 45 cal. automatic pistol. There were lots of metal springs, both coiled and flat, to pressurize and press parts in place. There were more moving parts than a real 45 would have had. I learned to assemble and disassemble those real 45s while blindfolded nineteen years later after I had been drafted into the army infantry during the Vietnam War.

I started trying to assemble the pistol about 9:00

p.m., after I was supposed to be asleep in bed. My parents did not check on me since I almost always went to sleep immediately. That night I wanted to put my new toy together. Even though I had a diagram to guide my efforts, the springs kept slipping out of place, over and over again. I persisted for over five hours, until about 2:00 a.m., when all of the parts finally stayed in place, and I was able to shoot wooden pellets. I still remember feeling extremely frustrated with what seemed like an impossible task. But, in my mind, quitting simply was not an option.

Truthfully, I do not know exactly why I was so determined. I do know that I had never given up accomplishing what I was determined to do. My parents thought I was a "strange child" in that regard, though they were both incredibly determined in their own lives. I never witnessed either of them quit in the effort to accomplish their stated goals. Perhaps I imbibed my determination with my mother's milk.

I learned to reinforce my determination by doing endurance-type athletics, particularly long distance running. There is almost always a point during these exercises when my body sends signals to my mind that it wants me to quit. I relish that moment because as I push past that point, my belief that "failure" is a choice, but never an acceptable one, is confirmed.

As you start building your dream life, whether your focus is on your career, your family, your health, your spirituality, or your emotional well-being, your life may actually seem more complicated than it was before. You will start to wonder why you embarked on this new journey when your old life was so much easier. You may even want to give up and go back to your easier life. But here's a tip: life is never, ever going to be perfect. As my mentor and friend Melissa West says, "Perfect is an illusion." If you think your life will be easy while it's under construction, you're wrong; if you think that after you accomplish your goals, everything will be effortless and you will never face new challenges, you're wrong. You're always going to have areas in your life that seem out of whack. As soon as you get a handle on one area in your life, you'll realize that something else needs your attention. For example, if you've recently created an exercise routine and lost ten pounds, you'll look up only to realize that your children need more time with you. This life of yours is always going to be under construction in some way. There will always be a new project to work on or a new challenge to face.

Especially when you are pushing yourself to become someone new, you must remind yourself that everything will be okay in the long run—even if life seems more difficult right now. Recognize that this is part of the process. It will pass. You will get through it. Be kind to yourself and others. If you realize that you feel differently about certain subjects, or that your thinking has fundamentally changed, don't allow yourself to feel lost—these are a part of changes you wanted for yourself. When you feel stressed or overwhelmed, remember that this is a part of your life journey: you are moving even closer to a life you will love. You will work through the rough parts and reap the awesome rewards that are waiting for you. You will soon lead a beautiful, fruitful life. You deserve this life. You deserve to be happy, fulfilled, and empowered.

# Designing Your Life: Questions for The Day You Want to Give Up

On the day you want to give up, make sure you come back to this chapter and answer these questions.

1. Why do I feel like giving up on designing a life I will love?

2. What happened specifically to cause me to feel this way?

3. What emotions am I experiencing? Am I fearful, anxious, angry, sad, mad, withdrawn?

4. What can I do to calm myself down? (Ideas: go for a walk, listen to your favorite music, hug someone, play a game, exercise, read a good book.)

5. How big is the problem I'm facing? Is it a five-minute, five-hour, or five-month problem?

6. Use these affirmations. Copy them down or recite them aloud.
    1. I am strong, confident, and ready to continue on this new amazing adventure.
    2. I am blessed.
    3. I am happy and at peace.
    4. I deserve this.
    5. I may fall, but I *will* get back up again.
    6. I can do this.
    7. I've got this.
    8. I have all of the resources I need to make this happen!
    9. I need to design a life that I will love. This is important to me.
    10. This energizes me.


7. Who do I need support from right now? What do I need these people to do or say to help me feel better? (Note: Be specific. If you need your spouse to tell you they believe in you, write that down and then tell them as much. If you need your mentor to simply sit and listen, note that, then tell them the same. Of course, you should always be willing to offer your own support when these people need you... because, certainly, they will someday.)


Today has been a very rough day, but we all have them. Congratulations on not letting your challenges get the better of you!

# 11

*Write Your Bucket List*

**Bucket list: noun, informal**

**A list of things a person wants to achieve or experience, as before reaching a certain age or dying: a bucket list for a terminally ill patient.**

**—from Annette White's *The Bucket List Journey***

In the midst of constructing your life, you'll start to come up with dreams, thoughts, and ideas that you never had before. Add these to your bucket list. Your bucket list is not just a list of things you would like to do in your lifetime, but a list of things *fully intend* to do. While your life is under construction, you should attempt to check off as many bucket list items as you can because you need to be trying new things right now. In this sense, your bucket list goals are similar to detours, with the difference being that detours are not always planned. Bucket list items are achieved with intention; however, there may be detours while you are in the process of checking an item off your bucket list, and that's okay too.

For me, one of the things on my bucket list was to drive up the Pacific coast in a cherry-red convertible. To force myself outside of my comfort zone, I let my husband plan the entire trip. I'm a bit of a control freak, so letting go of that much control was difficult for me.

Last June, we flew from the Midwest to California. After we arrived, we dipped our toes in the Pacific Ocean, which was a first for both of us. We ate at a really fancy restaurant that's often frequented by celebrities. We admired Santa Monica's majestic views.

The next day, we began our drive. We estimated it would take us about four hours to get to Napa Valley from Santa Monica. We checked the weather; it was going to be a perfect day for cruising in a convertible. We put the top down, turned on our Pacific-coast playlist, and went on our way. We were both so excited. The scenic views were gorgeous.

About an hour or two into our drive, we noticed that the road was becoming very curvy. We thought we could save some time by detouring onto the interstate. The next thing we knew, our four-hour estimate went out the window. The "shortcut" onto the interstate, which took us through a mountain range, stretched our driving time into eight hours.

In those extra unplanned hours, a strange thing happened: the detour became the trip itself. We laughed, listened to our favorite music, and saw breathtaking landscapes. I'm afraid of heights, so driving on the mountain roads and bridges (in a convertible, no less) became sort of a thrill ride. I will always remember that trip fondly.

As you start checking off things on your bucket list, remember that the journey may end up different from your expectations. That's part of the process. Not everything will end up as you anticipated. By way of example, I like to compare these twists and turns to being a new parent. Like most parents I know, I had a definite idea of what parenting would be like before I had kids. But when I *actually had* children, everything I "knew" about parenting went down the drain—which is beautiful in its own way because my children surprise and challenge me every day.

Maybe your bucket list involves meeting an influential person like Ellen DeGeneres or Oprah Winfrey. Perhaps it's about helping others in a way that you never thought possible, like volunteering in a developing country. All of these ideas need to be captured in your journal because they are part of the new life you are trying to create, but they should also go on your bucket list as well. To deny yourself these opportunities is to deny your personal growth.

When I was doing research for this chapter, I came across a blog called *Bucket List Journey* by Annette White. She is the author of the book *Bucket List Adventures*, the co-owner of Sugo Trattoria, and a serial adventurer. Her passion is checking off each item on her bucket list one adventure at a time—no matter where in the world her bucket list takes her.

As I was reading her website, I started getting extremely excited. Annette didn't just create a bucket list, she'd checked most, if not all, of her items off. She broke through her anxiety and fears and started saying *yes* to life. She has eaten insects in Thailand; swum with hundreds of jellyfish while in Palau (Micronesia); gone on safari in Africa; fed a stingray; zip-lined in the Costa Rican rain forest; kayaked with beluga whales in Manitoba; and even fed swimming pigs in the Bahamas. (Yes, that's right, swimming pigs.)

I felt there was no better person to talk about bucket lists and their importance than Annette. I reached out to her and asked her to share. I was a little apprehensive—part of me doubted that she would write back.

Overcoming my nervousness paid off: not only did Annette White respond, she has given me permission to share parts of her chapter "Creating and Conquering Your Own Bucket List" with you; the material below represents selected excerpts.

### Why Create a Bucket List?

*By Annette White, Author of Bucket List Adventures, Visit her at www.bucketlistjourney.net*

**Forces You to Look at What You Really Want:** Many people will live their entire lives without having any idea as to what they really want. They will follow society's conventional expectations of getting married, working the same type of job for the next twenty years, buying a home, and having children—all without giving it a second thought because that is just what they are "supposed to do." But, if that path is not their true passion, then life will end up leading them, instead of them leading their life.

The process of writing a bucket list forces you to take a close look at what it is you truly desire, to analyze where you are versus where you want to be. It very well may be the career, children, and home, etc., but it may also be something entirely different. We may believe that what we want is to have more money or to land that big promotion at work, but delving deeper reveals that what we really crave is more freedom and to be passionate about what we do. Will that new position at work really help you achieve your future goals or will it only stifle your creativity and keep you at work more hours of the day?

When sitting down to contemplate what your future will look like, your dreams and what type of experiences you want to have will be brought to the forefront. By asking yourself what you truly want, setting goals and consistently re-examining your goals, you gain a self-knowledge that will propel you in the right direction instead of focusing on random things.

**Motivates You:** Without motivation, your dream will be nothing more than that; it is the necessary energy that pushes you to accomplish your goals. If you think about it, most of the drive you have had in your entire life has been based on some form of a goal. You worked a part-time job in high school in order to afford a shiny new car, you suffered through endless piano lessons to be able to play at the year-end recital, and you ate salad for dinner every night in order to fit into a bathing suit by summer. Motivation is why race car drivers win trophies and business owners become millionaires, and it is the main reason that this is a published book, a project that took over a year and a thousand hours.

In order to truly get motivated you need to know what you really want, and writing a bucket list will help to determine exactly what that is. These goals will then be the root of your motivation. Also, having any sort of list naturally inspires you to want to cross things off of it, whether it is simply your weekly grocery-shopping list, daily to-dos, or a bucket list. Plus, having it written down will be a constant reminder of what you need to do, and will serve as the fuel that will drive you forward. This does not mean it will be easy, but once you set your list to paper and have announced it to the world, you have something to encourage you to push forward.

**Pushes the Boundaries of Your Comfort Zone:** It has been said that life begins at the end of your comfort zone, so then why are so many afraid of stepping outside of it? I will tell you why. Being inside your comfort zone minimizes stress and risk, keeping you at a low anxiety level. This makes it very easy to never push the boundaries, because it's pretty darn comfy inside the safety of your little bubble. Everyday activities like taking a shower, cooking dinner, and going to work don't create any apprehension because they are familiar. Whereas flying across the globe, eating strange foreign foods, and not speaking the language of an area will undoubtedly cause trepidation.

Unfortunately, if you stay inside of these boundaries you'll be missing out on the incredible benefits of taking a risk. It can lead to personal growth; expanding your mind-set, teaching you valuable lessons, increasing your confidence and limiting regrets. Your bucket list will continuously test these barriers, helping you to transform and grow. Once you step out of the norm for the first time, it can lead to a snowball effect, where each consecutive time you do it, it gets a little bit easier and your comfort zone expands bigger and bigger. That's when the world is truly at your feet.

**Makes You Feel Accomplished:** There is a new gallon of milk in the fridge, the children have taken their baths, and dinner is on the table. You sit back with a glass of Cabernet and relish in the success of the last eight hours. It feels really good to finish your daily errands, there is a sense of satisfaction knowing that you completed everything you set out to do for the day. Just imagine the triumphant feeling after you've walked the five-hundred-mile El Camino de Santiago or skydived over Palm Jumeirah in Dubai. The sense of accomplishment can truly be overwhelming.

Accomplishment gives you a feeling of pride, which in turn builds self-esteem and increases life satisfaction and fulfillment. When you are living the bucket-list life, you will be continuously making check marks next to your goals, and getting the addictive feeling of success often. It doesn't even have to be a gigantic long-term goal to benefit from the feeling of achievement; it can be as simple as learning how to make an origami crane or learning to ice skate. Plus, one of the best parts is that you are not waiting for someone to pat you on the back to tell you did a good job—it is a feeling you created yourself.

**Allows You to Dream Bigger:** Typically, when people create goals for themselves they are influenced by their current financial situation and personal time restrictions. They are usually thinking about things short term, instead of thinking of their entire lifetime. But, a bucket list is an invitation to dream bigger. When the time limit is before you die, instead of this month or year, it opens up the possibilities. It encourages people to put on it all the things they have ever thought about doing while taking away the limitation of fear, time, and money.

So make a bucket list and fill it with dreams that have no boundaries; things that scare the daylights out of you, make you pee-your-pants laugh, and inspire you to be a better version of yourself. Keep it close, refer to it often as a reminder to never forget your dreams.

## CREATING & CONQUERING YOUR BUCKET LIST

Sleep in an overwater bungalow in Bora Bora, hike Peru's Inca Trail to Machu Picchu, or drink beer at Oktoberfest in Germany—what's on your Bucket List? For too many people it takes a terrifying illness, hitting retirement age, or some other life-altering event to honestly begin thinking about the things they want to experience in their lifetime. In many of these cases, it will then be too late to turn these dreams into a reality. Life is uncertain, and you will undoubtedly be thrown curveballs throughout. You cannot be sure that in ten or twenty years you will be physically, emotionally, or financially able to do all of the things that you desire, like climbing the twelve-hundred steps of Sigiriya Rock in Sri Lanka or hiking between the cities of Italy's Cinque Terre. Don't wait for that "perfect time" to begin, create your bucket list not because you are dying but because you want to live!

There is no right or wrong way of designing a bucket list, no one specific prescription. It is a personal journey between you and your aspirations. Each one should be different because it is meant to reflect what you most desire in your own life. For example, mine includes learning to surf, skydiving, and rappelling down a waterfall to appease the adventurous side of me. If you are not a thrill seeker, your list may be entirely different. The important part is to come up with items that are meaningful to you; ones that will inspire you to wake up each morning with a fire in your belly. Retiling the bathroom has no place on this list, nor does cleaning the cobwebs out of the garage. Save those for your weekly "honey-dos." With that said, don't worry if you didn't make each aspiration earth shattering, or even travel related; sometimes the simplest goals are the most rewarding. Giving a blood donation took less than an hour commitment, yet is still one of my most gratifying experiences. Also, don't exclude anything just because you think it is too difficult or frightening as it is meant to stretch your comfort zone. Do the same for the things you think are too simple. As long as it has meaning to you it should be on your list, because even the smallest achievement can give us the feeling of a great accomplishment.

The length of your list is also ultimately up to you; there is no magic number of goals that should be on it. You cannot put limitations on something that is meant to unravel your dreams. I do recommend having at least twenty-five objectives to start, with varying levels of difficulty. They can be as small as hiking a new trail at a local park or as big as running a marathon—some will be checked off in a weekend, while others may be lifelong journeys. Including short-term goals that can easily be completed will give you a sense of accomplishment and help to keep you motivated for the ones that may take years. By continuously working toward (and checking off) your goals, you will turn the sense of achieving into a good habit.

Don't pass judgment on your own abilities. You will be surprised at what you can actually accomplish. People put limitations on themselves by thinking that they can't do incredible things or because the big picture of an aspiration seems so overwhelming. You need to dream big, go beyond the realistic goals, and put down everything that you have ever wanted to see, touch, and experience. Be realistic, but also understand that we are capable of doing so much more than we think we can. Don't think it is too silly, just write it down.

Speaking of writing it down, one of the most important steps in creating a bucket list is recording it somewhere. Sounds simple, right? But even so, most people miss this critical step. Recording your list represents a sincere commitment, turning them into tangible goals—doable aspirations to work toward instead of wishful thinking. Studies have shown that people are thirty-three percent more successful with achieving their goals when they write them down, share them with the world, and are held accountable with weekly updates. It's also very easy to forget all of your aspirations if you don't have something concrete to refer back to.

My first bucket list was created in a small, green, flowered journal, and then upgraded to a simple Word document. Afterward, it graduated to a multi-tabbed Excel file. Now my over an eight-hundred-item list is located solely online on my blog, which has been the easiest for me. Not only is it conveniently accessible, but it also holds me accountable by being visible to the universe. There are also many phone apps and online bucket list websites where you can record your list and share it with others.

Starting is the hardest part, so let's begin right now. Yes. Now. Living your own bucket list is as easy as following the Four Cs: Cultivate, Commit, Conquer, Celebrate.

## CULTIVATE

Once you have made the decision to create a bucket list, you need to start cultivating ideas. You're bound to have a few items that you have always wanted to do in the forefront of your mind, and immediately write those down. But, how do you come up with other incredible ideas? How do you know what's out there in the world to choose from? The following are different methods to stimulate ideas for your list.

### Write Your Eulogy

At a time when I was suffering from a serious case of the blahs, a close friend challenged me to write my own eulogy. I thought that was the craziest and most depressing proposal. Why would anyone want to think about his or her own death? The answer is that by doing so you can learn a valuable lesson about what you want your life to look like when you are alive. What legacy do you want to leave? What do you want to achieve? What would you want your friends to say about you and your life after you are gone? What does your ideal life look like?

### Create Categories

Breaking up your life list into different categories can make the brainstorming process much easier. This is also a great way to organize it once it starts growing. Divide a page into your selected categories and list at least five entries for each one. You will find that some goals fit into two different sections; that is no problem, just record it in one—the most important part is that it's on there somewhere. Following are only examples of categories, if you find many of your entries fall into a category not shown here simply create it, this is your list.

Local Experiences
Adventure
Career & Finances
Charity
Creativity
Education
Entertainment
Events
Family & Kids
Food & Drink
Just for Fun
Personal Growth
Nature & Wildlife
Sports & Activities
Travel (Local, Domestic, International)

### Use the Buddy System

Sometimes you can be gung-ho about goal-setting on your own and the ideas will flow easily, while other times you need a little help from your friends. Not only will they bring new ideas to the table, but also together you will be providing accountability and encouragement to each other. Connecting with like-minded people, especially if they share the same goal, can be a great support system to keep you motivated.

### Get Outside Inspiration

You have ventured deep inside yourself to find experiences for your list, now it's time to get some outside inspiration. In this modern day of television, Internet search engines, and social media, inspiration is all around you; you just have to be in the bucket list mindset to see it. Once you start cultivating ideas, your instinct will automatically be on high alert whenever anybody mentions something worthy of a spot on your list. It is similar to when you've finally determined your dream destination is Italy and everywhere you look you notice either people going there, mentioning it in conversation, or it being written about in magazines. This is because your subconscious mind is already thinking about it.

Until this mentality kicks in, you can get inspiration from browsing Pinterest boards, watching travel shows, subscribing to adventure magazines, reading blogs (like mine, bucketlistjourney.net—shame-less plug), searching specific hashtags on Twitter, etc. The inspiration possibilities are almost endless. If that's not enough to get your brain's juices flowing, you can also watch the movie *The Bucket List* with Jack Nicholson and

Morgan Freeman. Though [the movie] did not start the bucket list phenomenon, it did bring the term to the forefront.

### Revisit and Review Your List

Revisit your list in a week or a month to double-check what you have with a fresh pair of eyes. Do this while remembering that putting something on your list is making a contract with yourself. Ask yourself if they are truly your goals or have they been added to your list out of social expectations? Delete items that you added not because you wanted to actually achieve them, but because you thought they should be on there. Be brutally honest with yourself. What do you want to see, do, and experience in your lifetime? Just because everyone has bungee jumping in New Zealand on his or her list does not mean it has to be on yours, unless it is really something that you want to do. Don't fill it with aspirations of other people, unless it truly resonates with your dreams. With that said, make sure that it is not your fear speaking when you remove something from your list.

Remove anything that is impossible, truly impossible, not something that is frightening or seemingly undoable due to lack of confidence. If you are a woman, living in a Byzantine monastery on Mount Athos in Greece is not going to happen since females were banned in 1046. Competing in the NFL for a man over sixty with no athletic skill: I don't think so. I am a firm believer that I can do almost anything that I put my mind to, but I also know my limitations.

### COMMIT

You have already begun to stop the cycle by

writing your bucket list, now you must truly commit to living it. Commit by making a personal promise to yourself that will assist you in living your dreams. When I first decided to make my bucket list a priority in my life, this was the pact I made with myself:

I promise to never let fear make my decisions for me and to take one step toward my goals each and every day.

This commitment caused me to analyze every declined opportunity to see if the reason was based on fear. If it was, I forced myself to turn my no into a yes. It also caused me to be continuously making progress toward a goal by committing to doing one thing every day. It didn't have to be huge, on some days it was simply researching hiking trails and other days it was downloading a travel app to my iPhone. Maybe for you, you can only squeeze in a step every week. Whatever it is, make a commitment to yourself and stick to it.

CONQUER

Okay, so you have this incredible list, now it is time to do something about it. A bucket list is not helpful if all the goals just sit unfinished forever. It is time to start turning your dreams into a reality. Time and time again we hear people mention the wish lists for their lives, wide-eyed with an excitement in their voices, the crackling of the wheels turning in the brain and an overwhelming feeling of hope. It's a contagious feeling; one that you wish would last forever. Then what happens? Unfortunately, that thought needs to turn to action and that's where the need for "instant gratification" scores a touchdown while hard work is left to watch from the sidelines.

Taking on the entire goal seems like an impossible feat, so day-by-day the excitement dwindles until the goal is a distant memory like the wrinkle-free skin I had when I was eighteen. Don't worry, it's happened to me too. But, there are some techniques to making sure you are successful.

### Be Accountable

Want to have better odds at keeping the commitment you made to yourself? Hold yourself accountable. You can do this by publicly announcing the contents of your bucket list or at least your active pursuit of one of your goals—share it with your family, friends, and even a couple of acquaintances. Not only will your enthusiasm be contagious, sharing will make you feel obligated to complete a goal, as you don't want to be seen as the person who goes back on their word. After telling a few people, there is no doubt that someone like Uncle Mikey will ask you how you are coming along with "that bucket list thing" at your next family gathering. Either you will have an impressive adventurous story to share or it will give you the little push you need to get back on track.

I held myself accountable by starting a blog and letting the entire world know my intentions. Even in the beginning when the readers were few, *Bucket List Journey* held me accountable every day. People would email asking what I was doing next, or they would congratulate me on one of my ventures. Several have even invited me to assist in one of their goals. I have been invited to Thanksgiving dinner at the home of one of my readers, on a sexy Playboy-style cruise with a stranger (I actually went!), and even was sent a gift card to a restaurant in Portland when I announced my plans to go there. With each interaction, it pushed me forward and strengthened my commitment. I didn't want to disappoint the people who were counting on me, and I didn't want to disappoint myself.

### Deadline Your Objectives

Setting deadlines can help escape the "someday" syndrome, a common excuse for why you won't begin today because you will get to it someday.

If you are putting a deadline to your entire bucket list, then it's not really a bucket list by definition, because your lifetime is the deadline. What I can recommend is creating mini-lists within your list, for example:

- Seasonal Bucket List—Some items will only be able to be done in certain seasons, like seeing the tulip fields in Holland or dog sledding in Greenland. Each year, create lists for summer, winter, spring, or fall.


- This Year's Bucket List—Instead of making a New Year's resolution, on the rest of the year break your list down to the items you want to complete in the next twelve months.


- 30 Before 30; 40 before 40; or 50 before 50—Choose goals that you want to do before reaching a certain age.

## Start Today

The more you procrastinate the less likely it is that you will be able to do all the things in life you wish. Change that procrastination into determination by starting today. Make the first step of your chosen starter goal something you know you can complete within the next twenty-four hours. If your dream is to walk the Great Wall of China, begin by researching the best path if your wish is to learn to crochet a scarf, start by finding a nearby class or set of instructional videos. Don't wait for what seems like the "perfect" time, because that time is today.

Sometimes we try to bargain with ourselves: "I will take that dream cruise through the Alaskan glaciers as soon as ___." You can fill in the blank: when your child turns eighteen, after your business has a more efficient staff, or possibly when you are debt-free. This bargaining tool makes us feel that our goal is actually possible, but the steps to achieve it will be taken at a later time—someday. Someday is not a guarantee. It is never too early to begin, don't wait for that someday that may never come. Go at life with a curious spirit, adventurous soul, and fearless mindset.

## CELEBRATE

When you are working toward a goal there are bound to be challenges. Being so focused on the task at hand can turn these obstacles into setbacks, especially when you are not taking opportunities to celebrate small victories. When you reach a benchmark, stop to celebrate your progress. Let's say you check off booking your hotel in Switzerland today, then reward yourself with a delicious piece of Swiss chocolate.

After putting a big bold checkmark next to an item on your list, make sure that the incredible memories and powerful feelings related to them don't slip away. Keep a memory book filled with keepsakes, post photos on social media, or write in a journal. Do anything that will keep the memory alive and motivate you to achieve the next dream.

As I started my bucket list crazy things started happening to me. One night I woke up at 2 a.m. and had the idea to google 'empower women conference.' Where that came from I'm not sure, but I did it and found a Women's International Empowerment Conference. They were looking for speakers and I thought, "I should apply." I applied to speak about this book, *Life Under Construction*. I didn't think about it again for months. Then one day guess what happened? Yep, I got selected to speak at this conference and guess where it is? Thailand! The funny thing is one of my audacious bucket list items is to become an international speaker. Guess what I'll be after I go speak there? An international speaker! What? How cool and crazy. I promise things like this will happen to you too as you create your own bucket list.

Your bucket list will be as unique as you are, and it will likely expand as you start to grow. Use Annette's advice to get started. Initially, your list will probably just be a handful of items, but as you start to feel the accomplishment of checking each item off your list, you will become energized and want to do more. I'll be posting my own bucket list, on my site (www.allisonliddle.com) soon; there'll be a link on the page that you can use to email me your own bucket list stories as well!

# Designing Your Life: Questions for

## Write Your Bucket List

The following text is excerpted from Annette White's book *Bucket List Adventures*.

Sometimes the biggest "aha" moments come from asking yourself a question that has never been asked of you before. It can lead to overwhelming emotions and enlightening answers. Play a game of Twenty Questions with yourself to find what adventures you would be most passionate about. Asking yourself these questions will provoke answers that can determine the life that you want to lead. If you get stumped, just skip to the next one and come back later. Don't let your answers be controlled by fear or self-doubt, this is the place to dream bigger than you ever thought possible. Even I go back and ask these questions of myself from time to time, and as I have evolved as a person, so have some of my answers.

1. Where in the world would you like to visit?
2. If you had one month to live, what would you do?
3. What types of new foods do you want to try?
4. What cultural traditions are you interested in?
5. Are there any activities or sports that you want to try?
6. What events do you want to attend?
7. What has always been your biggest dream in life?
8. What classes have you always thought about taking?
9. If money and fear were not an issue what would you do?
10. Who have you always wanted to meet in person?

11. What would you like to do with family and friends?
12. In what ways do you want to improve yourself physically, mentally, or spiritually?
13. What skills have you wanted to learn?
14. Is there a charity you have always wanted to support?
15. What was your childhood dream—is it still relevant today?
16. If you won a multi-million-dollar lottery today, what would you do?
17. If you were on your deathbed, what would be your regrets?
18. What travel stories would you want to share with your grandchildren?
19. If you had three wishes what would they be?
20. Is there someplace you have always wanted to take your spouse, best friend, and/or parent?

# 12

*Trying Things Out*

"Do. Or Do not. There is no try." —Yoda

It's okay if you don't take Yoda's advice when you're designing your life because this is a time when you should be trying new things. A lot of new things. Things that may not even make sense to you initially. If you've thought about trying something new, and if that thought keeps popping into your head, don't fight it. Give whatever is interesting to you a try. Who knows, you might like it. And besides, what can it hurt?

When I was in fourth grade, my friend Amanda and I liked building things. One week, we decided we were going to build a motorless go-cart. We disassembled a couple of old bikes so we could use their wheels, and we found a long board to use for the go-cart's main body. But then we realized we were missing some key parts of the go-cart, like axels. This was a major construction flaw, so we gathered up the money in our piggy banks and took a trip to the hardware stone. I think we went up and down every aisle, laughing all the while. This was a new adventure for us and we were so excited about building our first go-cart.

After we found a few supplies that fit our meager piggy-bank-funded budget, we attached the go-cart's wheels to the thin rods we had bought to use as the axels. Then we attached the axels to the board. Now we were ready to go! Eager to try our creation out, we both clambered into our go-cart. Almost instantly, the thin rods buckled under our weight and we fell in a lump onto the ground.

We laughed so hard that tears rolled down our faces. We didn't care that we had failed, we were happy we had tried. It was a great day. And, if nothing else, we figured out how *not* to build a go-cart.

Sometimes the things we learn from the process of failing are bigger lessons than the stuff we learn when we're succeeding. As you are designing a life you will love, you need to take some advice from the fourth-grade version of yourself: think of something that you want to "construct" in your life, then just do it. It might work. It might not. Either way, it will be an adventure.

As we become adults, I think we become increasingly closed-minded. We'd rather have all the answers to a question before we even ask it. Life is not like this. You will never be one hundred percent sure of any outcome, so, why worry about it? Even if we fail, there will be a lesson to learn. When trying things out, try not to be too hard on yourself. Don't give into frustration or disappointment. When you finally come up with the one idea that works, it will emerge and be fabulous. You'll show it to others and they'll say, "Yes, that's it!"

§

When I was on my first job search just after college, I was trying to find work in a part of the country that didn't offer a lot of opportunities in my field. I knew I needed to try out something new. I have a family filled with educators along with a deep appreciation for teachers and the work they do, and in college I had often wondered if I would enjoy teaching. That's why I decided to "try out" teaching by becoming a licensed substitute teacher.

Let me tell you, I soon realized teaching in a school wasn't for me. There were many wonderful days and I loved the children, but I never had a passion for teaching—it just didn't hold my interest. I gave my best to the job, but I knew it wasn't for me. But the experience did lead me to a new path.

Think about the things that make you feel happy and excited inside. Those are the feelings you want to foster when designing a life you will love. Think about new paths that you believe might bring a similar level of excitement to you and try them out. Perhaps there's something you've always wanted to try—like a new class—but never got around to doing. Maybe there's a new career path that you find particularly interesting. I suggest finding ways of exploring these callings that don't involve too much of an investment before diving in full-on. If you're interested in a new career, maybe you could contact somebody in that industry and buy them lunch. Or even better, see if you can shadow this person in the office for a day.

Take time to do your research. In that process, note whether or not you are getting more and more excited, or whether this direction seems ordinary or boring. If you're getting excited, keep pursuing it—you may be on to something. If not, perhaps you should go in a different direction. This is not failure; figuring out what you don't want is sometimes an important component to figuring out what you *do* want.

As you probably figured out from the last chapter, Annette White, the author of *Bucket List Adventures*, is an expert at trying things out. Annette believes there are four major reasons why we should try new things. Trying new things makes us more interesting, keeps us active, helps us to create our legacies, and allows us to dream bigger.

## Reasons for Trying New Things

### Reason One: Makes Us More Interesting

Think back to the last time you met a really interesting person. Did this person do the exact same thing day after day? Most likely not. To be interesting, you need to try new things and create interest in your everyday life. You need to finally schedule that trip to Ireland or buy the running shoes you'll need for your first race.

As you start trying new things, you'll automatically become more interesting: when you're at a dinner party, you'll be able to discuss the fun and crazy things you've done in your life. Maybe you went skydiving or rode through the mountains in a convertible. Perhaps you wrote a book or traveled to Africa. All of these new and exciting adventures make you more interesting to others. Other people will be inspired by the actions you're taking in your life.

## Reason Two: Keeps Us Active

Each of us has a choice each morning: we can get out of bed and do something, or stay in bed and do nothing. It's the same with our bucket list. As we start trying more things, we will become more and more active. Maybe you've always wanted to learn how to do yoga or hike. Perhaps you want to try martial arts or sailing. Whatever it is, get out of that bed and *get going*. Trying new things and moving outside of your comfort zone will have added health benefits. Physically, your new workouts or activities will make you stronger; mentally, you will become stronger because you'll be seeing things from new perspectives; emotionally, you will most likely feel more confident because of all the new and exciting things you'll accomplish. All this will help you become a healthier person.

## Reason Three: Creates Our Legacies

When you reach your later years, what kinds of stories do you want to be able to tell your grandchildren? By sharing with them the stories of the time you went whale watching off Cape Cod or spent a month in France, you'll be encouraging the next generation to pursue their dreams as well.

Maybe whale watching isn't on your personal bucket list, but your own adventures will stretch you as a person, bring interesting new people into your life, and perhaps even give you the opportunity to help others. All of these things will become a part of you; they will build your legacy and become the story of your life. By sharing your adventures with younger generations, they will remember the very best of you and will be inspired by your example.

## Reason Four: Allows Us to Dream Bigger

As you check items off your bucket list, it will become glaringly obvious to you how much potential you actually have. You'll start to realize that you can do much, much more that you originally thought. This one realization will allow you to start dreaming even bigger. The bigger you dream, the more you will accomplish. And since a bucket list means no deadlines, you have your entire lifetime to explore your dreams. You will be living your life with purpose: your dreams will start becoming your reality.

The more things you try, the more you will begin to understand what truly inspires you. But remember that sooner or later, you're going to try something that just doesn't work. In fact, it may happen several times. This happens to everyone, and this is when a lot of people give up. Don't give up: the journey has just begun. You just need to keep digging. Eventually, something amazing will emerge despite the stuff that didn't work out. Try things out and push yourself; you'll be amazed at the results.

## Designing Your Life: Questions for Trying New Things

Are there some things that you've always wanted to try? Or have you recently come across an opportunity you find exciting? Right now, while designing your life, just go ahead and try them. Make a list and mark them off as you do them.

1. What idea keeps popping up into my head as my "next step to try?"

2. What is the one thing I'm afraid of doing right now? (Write it down here, then go out and do it!)

3. What did I love doing as a child? (Pick one thing you loved doing back then, but rarely do now as an adult. Write it here, then go out and do it!)

4. If I had a full day to spend with any one person on the planet, who would it be? What fascinates me about this person?

5. What is the last new thing that I tried? (Was it a new hobby, an exotic food, a class, a new travel destination?) What did I learn from this experience?

Trying things out is about experimentation, which will

help you identify new things that bring happiness into your life. Congratulations on trying something new!

# 13

*Congratulations!
You've Designed a
Life You Love. Now
what?*

> "When I stand before God at the end of my life, I would hope that I would not have a single bit of talent left, and could say, 'I used everything you gave me.'" —Erma Bombeck

I love this quote by the legendary author and humorist Erma Bombeck. Isn't this the purpose of life? To figure out what talents you have, then use them to the fullest in order to help the most people you possibly can?

When you are designing a life that you will love, you are using everything you have in the best possible ways.

You are taking your strengths, talents, skills, and interests and pushing yourself to create a life that is more than you could have ever previously imagined. Moving yourself out of your comfort zone. Doing something different. Taking risks. Failing often and trying again. Finding support. Growing yourself. Understanding that you are *truly* worth it. Taking it a day at a time. Doing this for you. Dreaming bigger than ever before. You are remembering that you are a unique, wonderful person and that we need you. You are amazing. The life you dream of is obtainable. It is absolutely worth the effort. You will achieve it. Believe in yourself.

Awesome, you did it, you took the initiative and made the effort. Well done. But now what? This is the end of our journey together, but just the start of your personal journey. You should now have a design for your life, and you should be ready to dive head-on into full construction mode now. My hope for you is that you take your time to enjoy the process.

One of my favorite quotes, which is often attributed to the philosopher Lao Tzu, is, "The journey of one thousand miles begins with a single step." At this point, you should have a lot of different notes, ideas, Pinterest boards, and other things to help you with your life's construction. Way to go! This was your first step.

As I was discussing this book with one of my coaches, Melissa West, we mused about how our lives will always be under construction in some way. It's a misconception to think that we will ever be finished; as Melissa said, "If you're growing, your life will always be under construction."

Remember that this is a journey to help you discover what you want in your life. There are many different paths you can take to get there. It is going to take time. A lot of time. Clifton Maclin, whose inspirational story I shared with you in Chapter Ten, once told me that as a young man, he was sure he would've had his life figured out by twenty years old. Twenty came and went, and he was surprised to learn that he didn't really know anything about life. Later on, as he was approaching sixty, he thought there wasn't anything left in life that could surprise him. Sixty came and went, yet he's still surprised often enough. This is to say, you will not have every answer that you want. This is a fact of life. Embrace it.

You have now put some serious thought and effort into your ideal life. Congratulations! I'm so proud and excited for you. You stuck this out and are now changing your perspectives and thinking differently about your life—that alone is a true accomplishment. Most people simply let life "happen" without giving a second thought to taking control, but you've seized this opportunity to mold both your life and yourself. This too is part of your first step. The first of many toward creating a life that you will love.

Now that you've put together your thoughts and ideas, all you need to do is start acting on them. Sometimes acting on our intentions is one of our largest hurdles. Robert Schuller, a pastor and author, once asked, "What would you attempt to do if you knew you could not fail?" Think about that: if you knew you couldn't fail, would you start doing the very thing that you're afraid of? I think you would. So just do it!

Your life is yours to design. You need to create a life that you love. One that makes you smile every single morning. One that, as you rest your head on the pillow at night, you feel proud of. You need to give this life your full effort. Go all out! Become the person you want to become, the person you know you can be. Do those things you've always wanted to do. Explore, create, discover. Be you!

Will you ever arrive at this perfect life you've imagined? Will it ever feel like you've achieved exactly what you wanted your life to look like? And in the process of your construction, how will you know you're even on the right track?

Truthfully, there probably won't be any grand revelations telling you you're headed in the right direction. More realistically, you'll find your cues in smaller moments. I had one of these moments recently, after years of designing my life. My son was out playing at a friend's house. My daughter was napping. All was quiet. I was cleaning up the kitchen when I felt a deep sense of satisfaction wash over me; it told me the direction I was heading in was the right one. I know I have a long road ahead and that in many ways I'm still at the beginning of my journey, but as I looked out of our kitchen window and saw the beautiful sunshine, I felt beyond blessed. I've taken many steps to become a better version of myself: they are working.

Another way that you'll be able to tell that you're on the right track is when you start to feel closer to your purpose. What's my own life's purpose? To be honest, I'm not entirely sure. But I know that as I was writing this book I felt closer to my purpose than ever before. I came alive in a new way. I was excited, really excited, about communicating with others through this text and possibly impacting their lives. When your direction starts to feel right, you'll know you're finding your purpose.

One way to help you identify your progress is to make some notes about where you are right now. Sometimes we keep trying to move forward without ever taking note of where we are in the here and now. Then, six months or a year later, we wonder if we've moved forward. By capturing a snapshot of yourself, as you are today, you'll be able to look back on your progress more effectively. After you've made your notes, it's time to dive in. Become your best self.

§

Now it's time for you to take action. Even if that action is just a baby step. Do something with those ideas! Maybe you could be acting on the one thought that keeps popping into your head, whatever it may be. Don't overthink it, just act. Acting—right now—is really that important.

When you start taking action, remember everything that you learned about change, and about yourself. Remember that you'll most likely face opposition. The journey will probably be difficult at times—so difficult even, that you may question whether you should even do it. At this point, remember that you're not alone—call on your support team and ask for some positive energy and guidance.

Be kind to yourself. Putting your life into true construction mode is a big deal, but the process doesn't need to be perfect. Doesn't it seem like you are your own worst critic? When that negative voice comes into your head, it can be difficult to ignore, but now you know how to shut it up! Listen to your laughing voice instead—it's the voice that will help you move closer to a life that you'll absolutely love.

Remember to take time for self-care, too. Read a book, have some tea, go for a walk, pet your dog, or do whatever makes you happy. When your life is under construction, it's important to stay in a positive frame of mind. You must practice self-care in whatever way you can. But above all, remember: you can do it!

## Designing Your Life: Questions for Congratulations! You've Designed a Life You Love. Now What?

Now, as you start taking action, know that your life under construction won't be perfect. But as long as you push through the tough times, you will always emerge stronger, more courageous, and have more to give others.

1. Have I taken a few moments to record where I am today?

2. What am I proud of? What am I striving to complete? What am I excited about?

3. What actions am I going to take right now, today, towards a life I can love?

4. If I were to write one sentence to a friend about designing my life what would it say?

5. How do I want to further transform my own life?

Are there specific areas in my life in which I want to see change and transformation?

Congratulations on starting your life under construction! I'm proud of you!

# *Afterword*

I thank you for allowing me to be a part of your life. Although we haven't met, I have thought about you during this entire book. I have written this book to speak into your life. I pray that it helps you move closer to a life you can absolutely love and is a resource for you that will help you move closer to your dreams. Even if we never meet, I hope you read this book again and again because I know it will be helpful in the different seasons of your life.

If you apply the lessons I share in this book, I assure you that you'll start achieving more in your life than you ever imagined; you'll want to pinch yourself to make sure you're not dreaming because so many awesome things will come into your life.

I know amazing things will happen to you because they happened to me while I was writing this book. Writing a book had been on my bucket list for a long time, but I never found quite the right inspiration. It wasn't until I began actively shaping my own life that I realized I could share my story and perhaps truly help others design a life they could love. As I started writing, I recognized that amazing people and experiences kept popping into my life. I couldn't explain what was happening, but I knew these people and experiences came to me because I was immersed in changing my life for the better.

Even if only one person reads this book and has one positive outcome, I will have done my job. That person may be my little sister or my little brother, or even one of my children. Or it could be somebody who I've never met, but relates to my story. It could be you.

Whoever you are, I hope you know how passionately I feel about helping you to design a life that you can absolutely love. A life that you imagine, design, and begin living. Because I believe wholeheartedly in your having a life that you love. A life that is lived intentionally and that makes you happy.

On your journey, I encourage you to visit my website www.allisonliddle.com. You will find many useful resources there to help you, but I also encourage you to email me and tell me your own life under construction story. I look forward to each and every one of your messages.

# *Acknowledgements*

*Life Under Construction* would never have been finished if Seth Godin hadn't encouraged me to "just do it" at the March 2017 International Maxwell Certification conference. Thank you, Seth!

I thank my husband Tony, and children, Logan and Avery, for being a part of my *Life Under Construction* story. I love you. To all of my family and friends who loved and supported me when my life was under construction: I am blessed to have you in my life.

I thank my mom Shari, my stepfather Rick, my sister Anika, and my brother Reid for their love and support through all of the construction that has occurred in my life.

I thank my extended family for being loving, kind, and teaching me so many life lessons. My Grandpa Paul Michels was one of my first mentors. My Grandpa Kenneth Kinner was one of the hardest working people I ever met—I used the tenacity I learned from him to fight through the days I wanted to give up. I'm sure they are both watching from above.

I thank all my mentors for teaching me so much and coming into my life at just the right time. John Maxwell,

Paul Martinelli, Mark Cole, Deb Eslinger, and Chris Robinson—I owe you each my gratitude. To my personal, individual mentors:

- Kellie George—thank you for being my positive encourager.
- Clifton Maclin—thank you for guiding me with your wisdom.
- Melissa West—thank you for believing in me before I believed in myself.

Thank you to the amazing authors who graciously gave their permission to have excerpts of their work included in *Life Under Construction*:

- Katy Caschera, president, Need2Be, Inc. and author of the *Personal Success in a Constantly Changing World*
- Clifton Maclin, member of The International Maxwell Certification and author of *Never Giving Up*
- Paul Martinelli, founder of The John Maxwell Team and author of the presentation *The 5 Mistakes of Goal Setting*
- Annette White, "Bucket list guru" and author *Bucket List Adventures*

Additional thanks to John Maxwell, author of *The 15 Laws of Growth*, Andy Andrews, author of *Storms of Perfection*, and to David J. Schwartz, Ph.D., author of *The Magic of Thinking Big*: without your empowering ideas and concepts, *Life Under Construction* would not be the same book.

Thank you to Erika DeSimone, my editor: I appreciate everything you did to help create this book. I thank my proofreader, Danielle Anderson, for her keen eye. And I thank all of the people who offered their insights as I navigated through the book-publishing process, especially my book launch team.

To my readers, I thank all of you for reading this book. God bless!

# *About the Author*

Allison Liddle is a certified John Maxwell Team keynote speaker, executive coach, and leadership trainer who is passionate about helping people thrive both personally and professionally. As an entrepreneur, she started her first business at age twenty-three. She then went on to found a national, award-winning financial planning firm called Prosper Wealth Management that has been featured in *Forbes* and USA Today. Allison is a lifelong Wisconsin resident; she currently lives in central Wisconsin with her family. *Life Under Construction* is her first book. You can visit her at www.allisonliddle.com.

# *Is Your Life Under Construction?*

©AttreoStudio

If so, you've found the person who can help! Allison Liddle has spent over a decade building successful businesses and growing herself personally. She has been privileged to learn about leadership and development directly from some of the world's top experts including John C. Maxwell. She has taken these lessons and applied them to her businesses, and to her life as whole. The results have been astounding. Today, Allison's leadership development focuses on her true passion—empowering others to design a life they can love.

With a winning style that includes a vibrant, upbeat personality combined with her knowledge of proven business-building techniques, Allison is the expert who will help lead you to success. She is available for keynote speeches, workshops, and coaching. Connect with her today at www.allisonliddle.com.

CPSIA information can be obtained
at www.ICGtesting.com
Printed in the USA
FFOW05n1518280817